SAILS, STEAMSHIPS & SEA CAPTAINS

Settlement, Trade and Transportation
of Island County between 1850-1900

Produced by Island County Historical Society

Sails, Steamships and Sea Captains
Settlement, Trade and Transportation of Island County
between 1850-1900

ISBN # 0-0929186-02-8: $15.95 softcover

Library of Congress Catalog Card # 93-77296

First Printing 1993

Clipper Ship Muskoka from original watercolor by Joan Brosnaham

Clipper Ship C. S. Holmes from original watercolor by Joan Brosnaham

TABLE OF CONTENTS

Poems

Photo Index

Map Index

Copies of Original Art

SEA FEVER - John Mansfield
From: "Piping Down the Valley wild"

I must go down to the seas again,
    to the lonely sea and the sky.
All I ask is a tall ship and a star
    to steer her by;
And the wheel's kick and the wind's song
    and the white sail's shaking.
And the gray mist on the sea's face,
    and a gray dawn breaking.

I must go down to the seas again,
    for the call of the running tide
Is a wild call and a clear call that may
    not be denied;
And all I ask is a windy day with the
    white clouds flying.
And the flung spray and the blown spume,
    and the seagulls crying.

I must go down to the seas again,
    to the vagrant gypsy life,
To the gull's way and the whale's way
    where the wind's like a whetted knife;
And all I ask is a merry yarn from a
    laughing fellow-rover,
And quiet sleep and a sweet dream
    when the long trick's over.

SAILS, STEAMSHIPS & SEACAPTIANS

ABOUT THE AUTHORS

This publication is a joint effort undertaken by a group of caring people who set out on a voyage of historical exploration. At various times they encountered both calm and stormy waters. Their effort was an act of faith, in much the same way as our Sea Captains voyages were when they sailed uncharted waters.

To the best of their ability they endeavored to present an accurate picture of life in Island County during the last half of the 19th century and to give a glimpse of native life before the arrival of settlers. They tried to give you a sense of the vision the pioneer forefathers held, of great towns, bustling harbors and important railroads. It was a time when the highways were the water ways: oceans, sounds and rivers. A time when boats, small and large moved commerce. A time before the train and the automobile changed that pattern forever, and hopes of great cities on Whidbey and Camano Islands died.

As a wilderness waiting to be tamed, this area offered opportunity and challenge. As a semi-urban area, the area today offers opportunity and challenge of a different kind. By studying the past we hope to find ways of preserving some of the abundance that greeted the early settlers, so we can continue to prosper and enjoy the beauty of Island County.

This book was literally done by committee, which will explain why it sometimes may seem to speak with more than one voice. To all it was a labor of love.

Our thanks to the following people:

Project Supervisor and Executive Director , Island County Historical Society Museum: Don Wodjenski

Coordinator/SeniorEditor/Writer: Judy Van Deen

Editors: Nancee Dickson, Karen Erbland, & Cynthia Kaul

Writers/Researchers: Kim Davis, Nancee Dickson, Karen Erbland Jane Jones, Cynthia Kaul, Pat Skud, Peggy Townsdin, & Herb McDonald

Maps & Illustrations: Cynthia Kaul

Nautical Advisor: Marshall Bronson

Production: Ray Davis and Vince Wray, & Janet Wodjenski

Cover Art: Sally Coupe Jacobson.

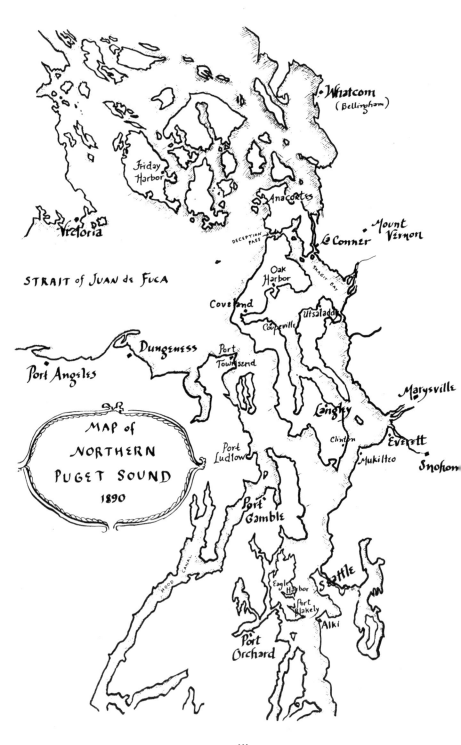

MAP of
NORTHERN
PUGET SOUND
1890

STRAIT of JUAN de FUCA

• Whatcom
(Bellingham)

Friday
Harbor

Anacortes

Victoria

DECEPTION
PASS

Le Conner

Mount
Vernon

SKAGIT BAY

Oak
Harbor

Coveland

Utsalada

Coupeville

Dungeness

Port
Townsend

Port Angeles

Marysville

Langley

Everett

Clinton

Port
Ludlow

Mukilteo

Snohom

Port
Gamble

HOOD CANAL

Seattle

Eagle
Harbor

Port
Blakely

Alki

Port
Orchard

iii

PREFACE

Whidbey Island, because of her timber and benevolent location, became a hub of commerce in the last half of the 19th century. A look at other events occurring during this period will put this into perspective.

1850	The population of the U.S. was 23 Million, 3.2 million were black slaves;.
	California became a state;
	Henry Clay laid his compromise slavery resolution before the U.S. Senate;
	The British, under Prime Minister Disraeli, were fighting the Sikhs, annexing Punjab, and developing Hong Kong;
	Hawthorne published the *Scarlet Letter*
1851	Herman Melville published *Moby Dick*;
	Isaac Singer invented the continuous sewing machine
1852	Harriet Beecher Stowe, published *Uncle Tom's Cabin*;
	Wells Fargo & Co. was founded.
1853	Samuel Colt revolutionized small arms manufacture;
	The Crimean War began when the Turks rejected the ultimatum of Czar Nicholas I.
1854	Britain and France allied with Turkey and declared war on Russia;
	Commodore M. C. Perry negotiated the first American- Japanese Treaty;
	Republican Party was formed.
1850-1860	424,000 people imigrated to the U.S. from Britain;
	914, 000 imigrated from Ireland;

1855	The first iron Cunard Steamer crossed the Atlantic;
1857	Royal British Navy destroyed the China fleet;
	Otis installed the first elevator.
1860	Lincoln was elected president;
	The first Pony Express rides left St. Joseph, Missouri and delivered mail to Sacramento in 10 days.
1861	Lincoln signed the Emancipation Proclamation;
	The Civil War began;
	The University of Washington was established in Seattle.
1862	The Merrimack and the Moniter fought the famous Civil War naval battle;
	Permission to build the Union Pacific Railroad was given by the United States Government, by an Act of Congress;
	The "Battle Hymn of the Republic" was composed;
	The Morrell Land Grant Act passed - 470,000 settlers applied in the next 18 years under terms of the Homestead Act.
1863	Lincoln dedicated the National Cemetery at Gettysburg;
	The Emancipation Proclamation was effective January 1;
	Free city mail delivery was established by the United States.
1864	*In God We Trust* first appeared on coins;
	The first salmon cannery opened in Washington, and California.
1865	The Civil War ended;
	Lincoln was assassinated;
	The Stetson 10-gallon hat was created
1866	The first cattle drive occurred over the Chisholm Trail;

Civil Rights Bill passed over President Andrew Johnson's veto;

Cholera killed 300,000 people on both sides of the Atlantic.

1869	The Suez Canal opened;
	The famous sailing vessel *Cutty Sark* was launched.
1870	The 15th Amendment to the Constitution was ratified forbidding the denial of vote for race, color or previous servitude.
1871	The Indian Appropriation Act passed, making Indians wards of the federal government.
1873	San Francisco cable cars began operation.
1875	President Ulysses S. Grant opened the Oregon Territory to white settlement.
1876	The United States Centennial Expo opened in Philadelphia;
	Alexander Graham Bell said, "Mr. Watson, come here, I want you."
1878	Ivory Soap arrived on the market.
1879	Congress allowed women to practice in the Supreme Court
1880	Los Angeles's population was 11,183 and growth limited by water shortage.
1881	American Red Cross was founded.
1882	U. S. immigration from Germany peaked.
1884	*The Adventures of Huckleberry Finn* by Mark Twain was published.
1885	The *Good Housekeeping* magazine began publication;
	The Boston Pops orchestra was founded.
1886	The last major Indian war ended with Geronimo's capture;
1887	Anti Chinese riots broke out in Seattle.

1889	Oklahoma Territories opened to white settlers.
1891	Carnegie Hall opened.
1893	U. S. Rural Free Delivery tested routes in West Virginia.
1894	The First Hershey bar was made.
1885	Columbia River Salmon cannery peaked at 634,000 cases.
1886	Queen Victoria celebrated her Diamond Jubilee.
1898	The *Battleship Maine* blows up in Havana.
	Sunset Magazine began as promotional material to attract tourists to California.
1900	U.S. Population reached76 million.

Chapter One

Coming of Man and Northwest Discovery

"Civilization is a stream with banks. The stream is sometimes filled with... killing, stealing, shouting and... things historians usually record, while on the banks, unnoticed, people build homes, make love, raise children, sing songs, write poetry and even whittle statues. The story of civilization is the story of what happened on the banks."

Will and Ariel Durant, authors of
The Story of Civilization.

Today it is hard to imagine the world that the Northwest natives inhabited before the white man came to the area in the last half of the 19th century. Perhaps by standing on the bluff above Ebey's Prairie a sense of how it was can be glimpsed. The major landmarks remain: Glacial, faintly smoking Mount Baker, which Isaac Stevens referred to as the northwestern pillar of the United States, rises to the northeast embracing the southern sound. The white mound of Mount Rainier looms and directly across Admiralty Inlet, dominated by Mount Olympus, are the jagged snow-capped peaks of the Olympic Peninsula, which shield central Whidbey Island from the full fury of the ocean storms, and protect her from the torrential rainfall to the south.

Fifteen thousand years ago, what is now known as the Puget Sound basin, was covered with glacial ice. For a period between 18,000 and 11,000 B.C., geological evidence indicates an ice mass nearly one mile thick covered the central and northwestern region of Washington State. A glacial mass known as the Vashon covered the region south between Chehalis and Olympia. Around ten thousand years ago, the slow grinding of the glaciers' gradual retreat carved the Puget

Sound basin we recognize today.

Archeological remains from earlier than 5,000 years ago are not abundant but evidence of humankind in the Puget Sound region between 7,000 and 8,000 B.C. exists. There is enough evidence from archeological excavation to prove that migrating peoples with tool-making abilities entered the area during this period and settled where fish, game, and vegetation were suitable for survival. These people brought tool-making skills, which when applied to local materials such as cedar, gave rise to a culture identified as Coast Salish. This culture could only have been sustained with superior water transport. The canoe was the only means of transportation that could move people and their belongings over the great distances traveled to hunt game and gather food.

In this inland Pacific waterway where the ancient forests grew to the water's edge, the people adapted to life along rivers, bays, and estuaries where food sources were plentiful and accessible. The waters teamed with various kinds of sea food. Mild climate produced a bounty of berries and other plant foods, and wild game was abundant.

The Coast Salish were the first mariners to explore the region and learn how best to use the tides and currents to propel them toward their destinations. These tides and currents in Puget Sound flow between two and nine knots, depending on the height of the tide and the distance between the shores in a channel. Tidal flow at Deception Pass, at the northern end of Whidbey Island, can reach nine knots. Fortunately, there is a period during the incoming tide at the mouth of the Skagit River when a canoer can actually use the incoming tide as an aid to gain an advantage over the down river flow and thus ease travel up-stream.

The Coast Salish used canoes of several different types. The largest carried large groups of people and material, and were also used in warfare. These Westcoast type canoes were between ten to 50 feet in length and up to five feet wide. The largest could carry six tons of cargo. These canoes were made from a single cedar log, selected and carved by village master

2

carvers. With the help of male family members and slaves, it could take over a year to fell, move, and fashion the log into a finished vessel.

A high bow, vertical cutwater (where the canoe initially "cut" the water) and a somewhat low, vertical stern distinguished the Westcoast type canoes which were most often used for open water travel. The Coast Salish traded with Pacific coastal tribes to obtain these canoes. The canoe-making skills of ocean going peoples of the Makah, Tlingit, Nootka, and Kwakiutil were esteemed by the inland waterway tribes.

The most common form of Salish canoe was smaller than the Westcoast type and was used for saltwater fishing and hunting. It was pointed on both ends and had a sharp tapering "cutwater." This canoe was generally ten to twenty feet long and about two feet wide, with a round bottom. A larger "freight canoe" or "woman's canoe", was used to move household goods and families when moving to seasonal hunting and gathering areas. This canoe was similar in outline to the Westcoast canoe but had less ornamentation.

People traveling the rivers used a "Shovelnose" canoe which featured a broad bow and stern, which was usually poled rather than paddled. Finally, for children and casual use by adults, there was a "knockout" canoe which had an identical blunt bow and stern, but was smaller than the "Shovelnose".

The central and southern Coast Salish tribes of the Northern Lushootseed language group had the greatest influence in Island County and Northern Puget Sound. The Squinamish, Swinomish, Kikiallus, Stillaguamish, Skagit, and Snohomish tribes fished, hunted and gathered along the beaches and forests of Whidbey and Camano Islands. Archeological evidence and cultural memory support the idea that Southern coast Salish, Suquamish, Duwamish, and Snoqualmie tribes, as well as tribes from as far away as the Queen Charlotte Islands (Haidah) and the Pacific coast (Makah, Quillute and Clallam) visited southern Whidbey Island.

The Salish, generally peaceful in nature, referred to themselves as the "People of the Canoe." Over the centuries they developed trade and communication with numerous tribes within and beyond their own language group. Although some Puget sound tribes were more aggressive than others, virtually all tribal groups feared the far ranging Haidah. Traveling hundreds of miles from the Queen Charlotte Islands, off the coast of British Columbia, fierce Haidah warriors raided villages and took anything or anyone they pleased. Arrow and spear points identified as Haidah in shape and geologic origin have been found in fields and along the shores of Whidbey Island.

When Europeans and Americans first explored this region they discovered a widespread, diverse culture which practiced and understood trade as well as warfare. The first Europeans to see the northwest coast of North America arrived in the 16th century. Driven by the imagined riches to be gained through trade with Cathay (China), the seafaring nations of Europe sought the fabled "Straits of Anian," or the Northwest Passage. Fifteenth century cartographers, who saw no serious hindrance in a lack of dependable information, conjectured that these straits must lie between the continent of Asia (also known as the countries of Anian) and North America.

As a result of the discovery of the Pacific Ocean in 1513 by Vasco Balboa, the Spanish claimed the entire Pacific Coast from Cape Horn to the Bering Straits. The claim included all of the Lands whose tributaries emptied into the Pacific. No Spanish records indicate sea exploration of the Pacific Coast further than Northern Mexico at the time Sir Francis Drake made his voyage in June, 1579. Aboard the *Pelican* (later refitted and renamed the *Golden Hind*) Drake reported he had sailed as far north as 48 degrees latitude (near the Strait of San de Fuca) but was blown back south by a ferocious storm to about 38 degrees north latitude (just north of San Francisco Bay), and from there sailed west for England.

Drake's incursion into "Spanish" waters infuriated the

Spanish court. A Spanish effort was launched to press for further exploration to claim lands never seen, much less imagined, by Europeans. Sailing under the flag of Spain in 1592, a Greek captain, Joannis Apostolos Phokas-Valerianou known to the Spanish as Juan de Fuca, reported discovering the Straits of Anian at 47 degrees north. Within a year he had delivered the same information to the British Admiralty, claiming to have discovered a land of friendly natives, gold, jewels, and other riches beyond imagination.

Nearly 180 years passed before Spain or England would again send ships to the northern latitudes of the northwest coast. In that time Spain had squandered the riches of its south and central American holdings in wars against the Dutch, French, English and Portuguese for control of the oceans and territory. Spanish attempts to colonize the west coast were funded by the Viceroys of Mexico. After passing most of the Central American riches over to the Spanish king, the Viceroys were not inclined to expend their remaining wealth on further exploration to the north.

By the mid 1740's word arrived at the Spanish court that the Russians had discovered the Straits of Anion and were now probably encroaching on Spanish claims. Indeed, Vitus Bering had crossed the gap between the Kamchatcka Peninsula and the Aleutian chain in 1741. However, it wasn't until the conclusion of the Seven Year War in 1763 that Spain, England and France would again consider it safe to attempt explorations of the Pacific. By the 1770's, Russia was sending men to the north Pacific coast to trade, survey, and explore. British ships ventured into the Pacific with impunity. Although the Spanish still claimed the Pacific coast, it could do little to hold the claim, even with the advantage of ports in Mexico. The area was simply to large to control.

Juan Perez, in the frigate *Santiago*, searched the Queen Charlotte Islands in 1774 for Russian intruders without success. Spain mounted a second expedition a year later, with the *Santiago*, under the command of Bruno de Hezeta, and the *Sonora*, under the command of Juan Francisco de la Bodega y Quadra.

Hezeta and Quadra sailed from Monterey, Mexico, along the West coast, looking for suitable harbors and rivers. Northerly winds hampered their journey, and the crews showed signs of scurvy. By May they were forced to put ashore near the California-Oregon border at about 41 degrees North, to find water and vegetables and were attacked by natives. Heavily armed, the crew managed to stay for ten days, gathering food and resting. The voyage finally reached as far north as the coast of Vancouver Island before the ravages of natives, weather, and ill health forced the expedition to return to Monterey.

The British reached the Northwest coast in 1778. Captain James Cook had left England prior to the news of Hezeta's voyage. With two ships, the *Discovery* and the *Resolution*, the expedition reached the Northwest coast in March at about 44 degrees north.

The Spanish became aware of Cook's voyage and ordered the Viceroy of Mexico to seize his ship or any other English vessel in Spanish waters. Luckily, Cook managed to avoid Spanish galleons by sailing out of view of the coast until abreast of the Oregon shoreline.

Offshore winds and stormy weather made close inspection of the coast difficult and dangerous, causing Cook to put out to sea to wait out the weather. Once the gales had subsided he set a northeasterly course. He sighted the coast again at 47 degrees north, at an opening to a harbor which turned out to be a low spot on the coast. He named a nearby promontory Cape Flattery for its promise of safe haven for ships. Overnight, gale force winds drove the expedition off shore where they remained until the storm subsided. The ships were blown north, past the Strait of Juan de Fuca, missed by Cook who believed they did not exist.

The expedition finally landed at Nootka Sound on Vancouver Island's western shore. Here they found good moorage and friendly natives who appeared unsurprised to see white men. The Nootkas were willing to trade food and sea otter pelts for any bit of metal. The captain and crews were welcomed guests of the tribal leaders. Cook assumed the Nootkas had traded with other tribes for the glass beads and the metal knives they possessed.

The natives wore what Cook believed to be valuable furs. He deduced that these people had had no direct contact with the Russians, who, known for their lust for furs and enslavement of tribes that could procure them, would have established trading posts.

Cook remained at Nootka Sound for a month, repairing his ships and replenishing his stores. By the time they sailed, most nonessential metal had been bartered away for sea otter pelts, food, favors of the native women, and Indian craftwork. The expedition continued north into the Bering Sea and Arctic Ocean, going further north than any other known European explorations. Cook then turned south toward the Sandwich Islands (Hawaii), where he was killed by natives in an incident over a stolen longboat.

The expedition continued on to China, where it was discovered that the Chinese greatly valued sea otter pelts. The crews traded the pelts for nails, hammer, saws and scrap metal. The Chinese purchased pelts for nearly $100 each, giving the crewmen more money than most had seen in their entire lives. The crew beseeched their ship commanders to return to Nootka for more trade. When the request was denied they threatened mutiny. The officers stood their ground, unsure of their responsibilities without Captain Cook and chose to return to England.

Word quickly spread throughout England and Europe about the potential for riches on the far northwestern shore of North America. By 1786, English merchants had sent five trade expeditions to Nootka. When the Spanish discovered the English in their waters they began claiming land and detaining ships.

Word of activities on the West coast soon reached the East coast of the newly-organized United States but had little impact on it's government. Events happening on the other side of the continent held little interest for delegates to Congress. They were most interested in decisions regarding states' rights versus a strong central government. However, the word and its implications did not escape the merchant class. By 1787, a group of Boston businessmen had formed a partnership to send an expedition of ships on a two year voyage to the Northwest Coast to trade for all the furs they could acquire and to report the news of their discoveries. The Boston expedition was led by John Kendrick aboard the *Columbia Redidiva* and its tender, the *Lady Washington*, under Captain Robert Gray.

Kendrick and Gray reached the Northwest Coast with little resistance from the Spanish. After their rendezvous at Nootka Sound and assuring the Spanish that the Americans were exploring for wood to make barrel staves, the expedition split up. Kendrick went north in search for furs, Gray sailed to the south. Gray sailed into the Straits of Juan de Fuca which had been discovered by British Captain Charles Barkley earlier that year. They found trading slim, as those coming before them had depleted the stock. Additionally, the coastal natives (being experienced traders) were no longer satisfied with nails and glass beads, and now demanded a more profitable barter with the whites. Experience among the coastal tribes with the unscrupulous traders had ignited a hatred of whites so strong that to kill whites or trade with them were equal options. With supplies running low and the season turning cold, the American expedition sailed for home by way of China and Africa. Upon their return to Boston, the ships were immediately refitted with better quality metal implements and trade items, and were off again to Nootka Sound with Robert Gray as Captain of the Columbia.

The events in Nootka Sound in 1789-90 caused international concern, especially between England and Spain who both claimed the region as sovereign property. By 1792, the Spanish had taken up permanent residence in Nootka Sound. Although they harassed all traders, they seemed more tolerant of the Americans. Captain George Vancouver, on the

8

refitted brig *Discovery*, was dispatched to the Northwest Coast by the British Admiralty to chart the Pacific coastal waters, prove the existence of the Northwest Passage, and settle the land dispute with the Spanish over Nootka Sound.

Vancouver arrived at the Northwest Coast in late March, 1792, equipped with earlier reports and crude charts of the northwest. Exploring the coast northward from central Oregon, Vancouver dismissed Deception Bay (the name given the entrance to the Columbia River by Captain John Meares) despite evidence of fresh water and river debris, as just a stream. The following day a sail was spotted which turned out to be Robert Gray aboard the *Columbia*, and the ships hove to to learn of each other's findings. Lt. Peter Puget was sent to speak with Gray. Vancouver himself disdained contact with a simple merchant American. Puget learned that earlier British reports of Gray's explorations of circumnavigating Vancouver Island were false. Gray did admit to having sailed eighty miles into the strait before returning.

Arriving at Nootka Vancouver entered into negotiations of restitution with Don Francisco de Eliza, over an earlier commandant's treatment of British traders, return of captured furs, and claims of the country. Although ordered by the Viceroy of Mexico to negotiate in good faith with the British who were prepared to go to war with Spain, Eliza feigned innocence and would not speak of such matters.

Vancouver put his stalled negotiations with Eliza on hold and left Nootka early in May of 1792 to continue his exploration and charting.

The British sailed immediately for the Strait of Juan de Fuca. After locating the opening, Vancouver traveled west to Dungeness then dropped anchor in Discovery Bay on the western shore of Quimper Peninsula, near Port Townsend. From there the expedition split the mission of charting among three longboats. Vancouver, Lt. Joseph Baker and the expedition's naturalist Archibald Menzies and crew were in one longboat; Peter Puget and crew in a second; and Lt. James Johnstone and crew in a third. Joseph Whidbey was assigned shore survey, but was often with Puget and his crew. Lt. William Broughton, captain of the *Chatham*, stayed with the ship to effect repairs and replenish stores.

The James Tuft *is a Barkentine, differing from a bark in that only the foremast was square rigged.*

Chapter Two

The Discovery of Puget Sound and Whidbey Island

From May 2 to June 11, 1792, the Vancouver expedition charted and recorded the names of promontories, bays, harbors, mountains and passages. The crews were ordered to devote every daylight hour to surveying, with only one break during the day for rest. Camp was to be made at sunset and crews were to be on the water before sunrise. The accuracy of the charts was checked fifty years later by the American Naval expedition led by Lt. Charles Wilkes and found to contain few errors. What errors there were delighted the Americans who were happy to give new discoveries American names.

The discovery of Whidbey Island was accidental and almost left for other explorers to find. By late May the survey had completed the charting of the southern area where the body of water south of the Tacoma Narrows was named Puget Sound. The area to the north of the narrows was named Admiralty Inlet. Each bay and harbor was surveyed and generally named for an English lord, high ranking member of the British Admiralty, or member of the expedition (excluding crewmen.) Puget and Whidbey had completed the survey of the eastern shore of Whidbey Island and the western shore of Camano Island, reaching Similk Bay, east of Deception Pass. Believing they had reached the end of a long inlet, the surveyors returned south to rendezvous with Vancouver, who was aboard the *Discovery*.

On June 2, as the party was returning, Whidbey wrote of finding a cove and describing it to Vancouver, who made this entry in his journal, "On each point of the harbor, which in honor of a particular friend, I call Penn's Cove, was a deserted village...the surrounding country, for several miles in most points or view, presented a delightful prospect, consisting chiefly of spacious meadow; elegantly adorned clumps of trees; amongst which the oak bore a very considerable proportion, in size from four to six feet in circumference.

"In these beautiful pastures, bordering on an expansive sheet of water, the deer were seen playing about in great numbers. Nature had here provided the well stocked part, and wanted only the assistance of art to constitute that desirable assemblage of surface, which is so much sought in other countries, and only to be acquired by an immoderate expense in manual labor.

"The country in the vicinity of this branch of the sea is, according to Mr. Whidbey's representation, the finest we have yet met with, notwithstanding the very pleasing appearance of many others; its natural productions were luxuriant in the highest degree, and it was, by no means, ill supplied with streams of fresh water.

"The number of its inhabitants he estimated at about six hundred, which I suppose would exceed the total of all the natives we have seen. The other parts of the sound, did not appear, by any means so popular, as we have been visited by one small canoe only, in which there were five of the natives, who civilly furnished us with some small fish..."

On June 4, the *Discovery* and *Chatham*, with all crews aboard, met in Everett harbor, where Vancouver made claim for the British Empire on the lands and waters his expedition had surveyed. From Possession Sound (where possession of the region was taken in the name of the King,) the expedition continued out of the Sound and proceeded into the San Juan Islands.

As the ships dropped anchor, Whidbey requested permission to explore some of the small bays sited on the northward tip. In a longboat, he entered Deception Pass from the west, sailed through on an incoming tide and found himself in an area he recognized as having seen a week earlier. The discovery of a new island prompted Vancouver to name it after Whidbey. If not for the keen eye of Joseph Whidbey and fortuitous timing of the incoming tide, Whidbey's Island might have been left for someone else to discover.

Chapter Three

A NEW ERA DAWNS

Suquamish village fishing camp with long house

NATIVES

Early explorers sailed along the Northwest Coast in their huge- square rigged ships. Among them was 34-year-old Captain George Vancouver's three-masted sloop of war *H.M.S Discovery*, in 1792. He and his crew were the first to chart the deep bays and channels in the sheltered inlets of Whidbey and adjoining areas.

Then by sail and oar came the fur traders, especially those of the Hudson Bay Company, who were eager to barter with native hunters, and missionaries like Father Blanchet. They canoed to Whidbey Island in May, 1840, at the request of Chief Netlum (variously referred to as Netlan, Snetlum, Snakelum) of the local Skagit Tribe.

Later, with rifles, came the treaty makers, personified by Isaac Stevens, who hurriedly met with 2,500 natives, including the Whidbey Island Skagits on the site of present day Mukilteo, in January, 1855, to negotiate the Treaty of Point Elliott. This treaty ended any Native American land claims in exchange for promises of total care on the reservation near present-day Marysville.

The Oregon-Washington Indian War broke out between November 1, 1855, and August 30, 1856, because of efforts by the government to deprive the Indians of their lands before they realized the value of gold found in Colville, on the Columbia River, that same year. Whidbey Island responded by creating a company of fifty local volunteers, who called themselves the "Northern Rangers," officially Company I, 1st Regiment of Washington Territory Volunteers. Their commander was Colonel Isaac N. Ebey. They suffered no fatalities.

Ebey invited the friendly Skagit Indians on the Skagit and Snohomish Rivers to sit out the war on the Island, before river blockades were established as part of the strategic defense of the lower sound. One thousand fifty Skagit, Lummi, Nooksack and Samish Indians collected at Miller's Point to the north of Penn's Cove, and seventeen hundred Snohomish Indians camped at Skagit Head at the south end of the island.

Between the constant fear of Haidah Indian raids from the north, rumors of hostile up-river and Yakima Indians who might invade, and the increased irritability of the "friendly" natives camped at Penn Cove and Holmes Harbor after an attack by native tribes on Seattle in late January, Whidbey Island settlers nervously built block houses, and prayed their soldiers could stay home. Several of these block houses are still standing, one next to the museum in Coupeville..

During the war, the men who were away were mostly bored, and the women left on the farms were overworked and constantly worried. Crop yields were down that season, and additional territorial taxes were levied to pay for the war.

Waves of pioneer settlers came, as irreversible as the tide. Many were sea captains, ready to "swallow the anchor" and build a home for their families. They invested in local commercial enterprises such as a sawmill, or small ship building operation. Others were midwest farmers delighted with the rich soil and misty rains. Some were European homesteaders, who saw Puget Sound as a haven offering political freedom. Others were frustrated survivors of depleted gold fields from California to Alaska, who decided to look for the green gold of Puget Sound's forests and fields. They were a mixed bag.

This region became, in the 19th century, a crossroad of maritime world commerce, connecting sea lanes from London and Boston, to California and Alaska and on to Canton where furs and spars (tree trunks with bark and limbs removed) were traded for the treasures of tea and silk from the Far East.

Physically and culturally the Northwest would never be the same. The coast tribes were involved in mercantile and commercial ventures before the white man and readily accepted their role in the new trading business. They believed that increased business meant greater native wealth and material prosperity. The intial commercial call to the Northwest was for furs, especially the sea otter, not plentiful in Puget Sound but found north and south on rockier sea coasts. The quality and sheer beauty of the sea otter pelt was unexcelled by any other fur bearer and was approached only by its fresh water parent the land otter. In terms of currency, its value was unsurpassed, particularly in China. Bartered from natives with a few dollars worth of knives or blankets, a single pelt might bring up to a thousand dollars. Inevitably, after a few years of over harvesting of pelts, the fur trade failed, and the Indians became poorer every year.

The white man, unwittingly, brought diseases that natives had no immunity to fight and that ravaged them as no other enemy could. It was estimated that the Indian population of the Northwest coast fell from around 188,000 in 1774 to about 38,000 in 1874. Syphilis and tuberculosis were the most common afflictions among the Chinooks. Other diseases that raged at epidemic levels were smallpox and measles, breaking the back of the native resistance to Euro-American encroachment, both territorial and cultural

Still, the Indians traded and sold fish to explorers and settlers. They remained the primary fishermen of the area until statehood in 1889. The main course on the seafood "menu" was salmon. Five kinds of salmons are native to the northwest: Sockeye, Chinook or King, Coho, Humpback and Chum. In those early days the fish were so abundant when Vancouver came he found the Indians pulling them out of the Sound with crude nets made of bark and young willows.

GOLD

Gold, like otter pelts, had a major but indirect impact on Puget Sound and Island County. Neither were part of the Puget Sound's bounty but major discoveries elsewhere produced a demand for products abundant in the Puget Sound area; timbers of every cut, coal, farm products, and salted salmon. Boats of sail and steam were busy up and down the coast.

Of interest to pioneers on Whidbey Island was the gold strike near Fort Colville on the east bank of the Columbia River in 1855. Several local men were infected with gold fever and were preparing to join the rush to the mines east of the Cascades but postponed their trip after a sermon given by Reverend Morse at Isaac Ebey's father's house on September 16. Six days later word came to the Island from Seattle that two men had been murdered by Indians on their way to Colville. Three of the men who had prepared to go prospectiing were John Alexander, John Crockett, and I. J. Powers, County Commissioners of Island County, which at that time included the San Juans. They were probably spared by the delay.

Gold strikes contiued throughout the 1860's, spreading into satellite rivers of the Fraser, like the Thompson, Okanogan, Peace and Stikine. Puget Sound buzzed with supportive activities until 1864 when the Fraser River gold was gone. Many merchants and steamboat operators servicing the staging areas went bankrupt. A revival of the boom arrived with the discovery of gold on the Cariboo River, in 1856, in the Cariboo Mountains of southeastern British Columbia. This made Port Townsend the main jumping off port.

But these new strikes petered out and the nation experienced a series of depressions. Then on August 12, 1896, George Washington Carmack while fishing at Rabbit Creek discovered the Klondike Bonanza, on the Klondike near the confluence of the Yukon River in Alaska, and once again the rush was on.

This last great strike was a financial boon to a nation just coming out of a long depression. Most of all it was a blessing to Seattle and the entire Sound, all of which had an effect on Island County.

Seattle changed from a struggling lumber port to a thriving commercial and supply center with rail connections east and sea water transport around the world. Bank deposits surged from $4.6 million in 1897 to $12.3 million in 1899. The twentieth century had arrived on Puget Sound.

AGRICULTURE

Agriculture was a key element in the Puget Sound economy from the beginning. The Hudson Bay company encouraged growing food crops for trade with the Russians living to the north and with other trading posts not blessed with the rich soil and mild, moist climate found here.

From the early 1850's, the fertile plains of Whidbey Island provided commercial vegetables, greenhouse tomatoes and berries wherever ships could carry them. In 1852 John Alexander brought the first large load of domestic animals to the island, and soon beef and milk were added to venison as an Island-to-Sound export item. Pigs and cattle ran loose, but milk cows and draft oxen were fenced. By 1853 Colonel Walter

17

Crockett, Sr. had harvested his first crop of wheat on the Island and near a hundred bushels of onions, worth $6 per bushel. Isaac Ebey's Prairie became one of the most productive famlands in the United States.

In January 1864, Louise Swift, wife of Captain James Swift, described her kitchen budget: three cents per pound for deer meat, 50 cents for a goose, 25 cents for a partridge, six to eight cents a pound for beef, eight cents a pound for pig, 16 cents per pound of sugar, $1 a pound for tea, $8 per barrel of flour and 50 cents for a pound of butter.

As the area grew, Coupeville and Langley docks creaked with the movements of produce for Puget Sound ports. Potatoes were grown by Chinese farmers, until vigilantes ended their tenancy; sacks of wheat harvested by the Dutch brought record-breaking yield of 117 bushels per acre in 1892, before soils were depleted. For a brief time in 1868 a gristmill was established at the head of Penn Cove by James Buzby. By the 1870's, due to market changes, sheep farming took over for a decade and then it was back to potatoes and grains for island farmers.

To early settlers interested in dairy farming, the Puget Sound area was ideal. Climatic conditions closely approximated those of the best dairy countries in northwest Europe. The lowlands of western Washington between the Cascades and the coastal mountains remain the prime dairy region of the Pacific Northwest. This is evident today on Whidbey Island, which still has many fine dairy farms.

TIMBER

Lumber, from the beginning, was the spine of Puget Sound commerce. Captain John Meares took the first load of spars from the area in 1788. It was a load that never arrived because he hit a fierce North Pacific storm and had to jettison the cargo to save the ship. A Puget Sound spar was even installed on Captain Vancouver's ship *Discovery* in 1792.

Real development of the lumber industry started in earnest after the 1849 California gold rush, with little mills popping up in hidden bays and coves around the Sound. All were recognized by their muddy rows of shacks for mill workers and their families. Alongside many mills were small primitive shipyards. Among these sawmills was the mill at Utsalady on the northern tip of Camano Island.

Until the 1880's Puget Sound trees, often 200 feet tall with a twelve foot girth, were cut with axes and the logs hauled to nearby mill sites either by water or pulled by teams of oxen, often as many as a dozen, over crude skidroads. Skidroads were formed of short paralleled timbers imbedded in the ground and greased with dogfish oil.

Many mills and ships went up in flames and forest fires, usually started by lightning, often burned for months, leaving a polluting pall of thick smokey fog.

On Penn Cove, in the early 1850's, Lawrence Grennan, with partners Thompson and Campbell began exporting pilings to San Francisco. From the profits and the sale of salted salmon, he purchased 160 acres on north Camano Island from S. D. Howe in 1853. A stand of pristine Douglas Fir grew down to a deep anchorage. He ordered sawmill equipment from San Francisco which was lost on the Columbia River Bar. Grennan received credit for his order, and joined forces with Thomas Cranney's store and sawmill at Utsalady.

In 1855 supplies for Cranney's store were brought north from San Francisco on the bark *Anadyr*, owned and commanded by Captain James H. Swift of Coupeville. Outbound the ship loaded a full cargo of Utsalady spars for Falmouth, England and Brest, France; the first full cargo of spars exported from the sound. By 1857 they had built the frame for their sawmill and were loading shipping wood bound for Holland, France, Spain, China and as far away as the sugar producing islands of Mauritius in the Indian Ocean.

In 1857-58 they provided spars to the American, British and French navies. Their spars were indeed world famous.

Some were up to 125 feet long, 50 inches in diameter at the stump and weighed up to 20 tons.

Over a thousand men were working in a score of Puget Sound sawmills by 1869 with 170 million board feet of lumber cut that year. Also, there were on Puget Sound 113 ships, 491 barks, 45 brigs, and 87 schooners being loaded for California, New England, the Sandwich Islands, Australia, China, the Far East, East Indies, South America, Europe and Russia. The area was truly an international hub.

Map showing Native tribal boundaries.

21

Chapter Four
Whidbey Beckons

"The Land...is most grateful to the eye...rising in small hillocks and mounds till the more inland parts.

"It is overlooked by lofty snow mountains and indeed nature as if she studied the convenience of mankind, has so disposed of the trees as to form on the rising grounds the most beautiful lawns on which I have seen grass man height. Little would the labor be in its cultivation. An Island distinguished in the general chart by the name Whidbey's Island is absolutely as fine a tract of land as I ever saw, at least apparently so."

Quote from writings of Peter Puget

EARLY SETTLEMENTS

Ships bound for Puget Sound entering the Strait of Juan de Fuca found Whidbey Island displaying its bounty to the passing maritime traffic. To potential farmers Whidbey's lush rolling prairies offered appealing relief from the endless forests.

Word of mouth in San Francisco and Olympia advertised it as the garden spot of the Sound, a bread basket in the midst of forest and ocean. The deep water harbor at Penn Cove attracted many ship masters who would return to settle. They were impressed with the abundance of oak and Douglas fir for shipbuilding, masts and pilings. The clear meadows and the possibility of emigrating by ship ordained that the Island would be settled by families sooner than other outposts.

There are interesting accounts of settlers' journeys, of whaling and the East and West India trade which had sired a great fleet of sailing ships in New England and Nova Scotia. In the late nineteenth century, huge fully-rigged ships were racing "round the Horn" with loads of grain. The California Gold

Rush added cargoes of prospectors and supplies bound for the west coast. Many ships came to Puget Sound for cargos of Douglas fir spars for masts in Europe and the East coast, giving sea captains a glimpse of the area. Seafarers came via steamship to Panama and San Francisco, and when they were disenchanted with the gold rush, or city life, many came on to Puget Sound.

TRAVELING TO PUGET SOUND

The trip around Cape Horn often took four to six months, so many travelers chose the route over the Isthmus of Panama, which appeared easy, taking only a few days. Traveling by unreliable river craft, or by foot and pack mule through slippery, steamy jungle inclines, contending with graft, dealing with extortion for bad services, as well as discomfort and disease made the trip less than pleasant.

Services of the "lazy" native packers, boatmen and hotelliers had been preempted by American profiteers, described as "a mongrel crowd who brought disrepute to Americans," and charged exorbitant prices.

Mary Jane Robertson travelled in 1851 with her five children to San Francisco to meet her husband Captain John Robertson. Her granddaughter wrote a description of the journey.

"They boarded the *Brother Johnathon'*...and set sail from New York for the Isthmus of Panama. After nine days of sailing, the Brother Johnathon arrived at our point of debarkation on the Isthmus at the mouth of the Rio Charge's....The passengers ...found themselves in a native village of bamboo huts. Many old maps either show no name or mark simply, Fort San Lorenzo, as the locations.

"Here the ship's passengers had to bargain with the natives to pole them up river in flat-bottomed canoes to Cruces ...meaning crosses. ...many crosses along the way they traveled marked the graves of those who could go no further.

"The Isthmus is thirty miles at its narrowest point, so

regardless of who tells the story, it was a long, difficult and uncomfortable passage, not to mention having five children between the ages of nine and fourteen years to keep from harm's way."

When the emigrants finally arrived dirty and exhausted in disease ridden, chaotic Panama, they sometimes had to wait weeks and haggle for passage on a steamer going north.

In 1855, the Panamanian "tin train" went through and travel was cut to three hours from coast to coast. Even so, many privations and uncertainties awaited between Panama City and Puget Sound.

EARLY SETTLERS OF WHIDBEY ISLAND

In the early days of settlement, ships played the role of post office and store, bringing news from the outside world as well as offering passage to and from the Islands. Some "trade boats" sold specific merchandise, such as apples or chickens, while others were floating general stores. Currency was scarce and merchants were accustomed to taking other products in trade, like hand split cedar shakes, dogfish oil, potatoes or fur pelts.

The settlers were always happy to greet the boat, receive mail, exchange gossip and read some newspapers. Some vessels carried spars and square timbers out of Penn Cove for the San Francisco docks, and provided merchandise wholesale (often liquor), to small trade boats called plungers. Captain Barrington's *Growler*, built in 1858 on Whidbey Island, was one of the earliest and most successful of the trade boats.

Isaac Ebey came to Whidbey on the brig *Orbit* in 1850. He discovered, at what was to become Ebey's Landing, a fertile, nearly level prairie, surrounded by trees, with a crescent beach that offered sheltered anchorage. Writing to his brother he said, " this is almost a paradise of nature. Good land for cultivation is abundant on this island...." The landing, in a semi-sheltered cove, protected by Admiralty Head, became a port for many ships coming from Port Townsend, Seattle, Everett and as far away as the Columbia River.

Isaac Ebey and Samuel Crocket, family friends, brought their families west. Both men had a tradition of respect and mutual aid that sustained them through earlier frontier ventures in Missouri. The Oregon Donation Land Act was passed by congress on September 27, 1850. Eighteen days later Isaac N. Ebey, taking advantage of the provisions of this measure, came to Whidbey Island and filed his claim on the western shore of Central Whidbey.

Ebey's Prairie became one of the most productive farmlands in the United States. In 1850 Isaac wrote to his wife Rebecca, who had not come over the Oregon Trail to join him: "If you could see my potatoes, onions, carrots, cabbages, parsnips and peas, it would almost make your mouth water." The next year Rebecca tasted the vegetables, but died in 1853 at the age of thirty, four months after her third childbirth She became the first tenant of Sunnyside Cemetery in Coupeville.

Ebey was a natural leader and very active in local society and in territorial politics. He and several other islanders served in the Indian War 1855-1856, , which for the most part spared Whidbey and Camano.Islands.

Ironically, despite this lack of involvement in the war, Isaac Ebey, on August 11, 1857, was rousted from his bed by shouts, taken from his home and murdered by northern Haidah Indians, in a grisly retribution for one of their chiefs killed by the white men. By stealth, a drunken band of Kake Indians from the Haidah tribe slipped up a draw from the beach at Ebey's Landing, captured Ebey and killed and beheaded him. Many years later the head was reclaimed and buried with his body.

Today the 17,000 acres of Ebey's Prairie is still being farmed, its beauty unmarred and protected as a National Historical Reserve for future generations. Colonel Ebey's farmhouse still stands, and his fields are still being tilled.

While most settlers came by ship to Whidbey Island, many

came across country by prairie schooner. The great migration to the Oregon Territory is chronicled in the *Narrative of Samuel Hancock* a pioneer who eventually settled near Fort Casey

Like many immigrants on the West coast, Margaret and Isaac Power's parents had pioneered in the mid-west. Their children continued moving west, first to the Willamette Valley where they were involved in farming, lumbering, shingle making and some Rogue River mining. With flexibility, fortitude and perseverance in their search for a real home they made a last move by raft and skiff to settle on 640 acres on Penn Cove, where they logged and farmed.

Isaac had a blacksmith shop, and was one of the first Island County commissioners. After his death in 1859, his widow, Margaret, distinguished herself by managing the large stock and grain farm, and raising their children.

Dr. John Coe Kellogg and his wife Caroline also came by wagon train to establish a homestead near Admiralty Head and the first "hospital" on the Island. Known as the "Canoe Doctor", he traveled by land and sea to treat his patients. He was known for his compassion as well as his efficacy as a doctor and farmer. He was the first to bring the McCormick reaper to the Sound.

Early in their Island life he traded Caroline's silk shawl to a colleague in Olympia for a pig. A sea captain, delivering the sow, pushed it overboard off Admiralty Head, leaving the pig to get to shore by itself. Kellogg didn't hear of the pig's arrival for two weeks. He searched the shore and found her and 12 piglets thriving under a log on the beach. Later he brought 50 sheep ashore in the same manner. John and Frances Alexander also came overland, suffering many hardships along the way. These included difficulties with the natives and a crude leg amputation which would eventually cost John his life.

In the winter of 1852, nicely settled on Whidbey, Frances Alexander gave birth to the first white boy born on the Island. He was a great curiosity to the Indians. All day long after her trauma of childbirth, members of local tribes paraded through the cabin to see this wonder, bringing in the snow and wind. The poor woman was terrified and later said she hardly remembered the bitter cold.

Some time later, John was out on the beach in a storm and got his pegleg trapped between logs. He struggled free, but caught pneumonia and died. The struggle with life and death was always near as medicine was crude and not readily available. After his death, Frances earned her living for many years cooking for the men in the harbor. Later she married Captain Robert Fay. Eventually "Grandma Fay" and her son ran a hotel in Coupeville.

The Races, who still live on Race Lagoon, were descended from seafarers who emigrated from Australia and Tasmania, where Hobart Race's great-grandfather was in charge of a prison colony. The dynasty began in this hemisphere with Henry and Frances Race. He had been a California gold seeker in '49 and returned to Australia for his family. They lived in Port Gamble for 18 years before moving to Whidbey Island. Their brood of six children reflected the geography of their migrations: Henry Melbourne, Tasman, Austral, Frances Puget, William Hobart and Ronald James. Henry and Frances were very involved with education, music and the cultural life of Whidbey in the '80's and '90's.

Their son F. Puget, the druggist, married Hattie Swift, daughter of Captain James Swift. "F. P" was an honorary Skagit Chief, and the natives held potlatches and informal gatherings at the Race house at Fairhaven above Race Lagoon. Hattie and her sister exchanged household and gardening wisdom with the squaws for valuable information on dyeing, weaving and other native lore. Hattie was also knowledgeable about medicine and drugs, often assisting her husband in the pharmacy.

The home was later moved to Coupeville by her son, George Albert Kellogg, who had spent many happy hours listening to old Island tales told by Hattie Swift Race. He used this material to write a history of Whidbey in 1934. Hastie is another pioneer name that survives to this day. The family had sailed from Liverpool to New Orleans, then up the Mississippi on a riverboat. After living for a while in Wisconsin, they joined a wagon train west. As a young man Thomas had already been exposed to cholera, Indian raids, and quite a few hardships of the road. He was active in Thomas Cranney's logging operation at Utsalady and left a powerful mark on the Skagit Delta and Whidbey Island.

In 1851, three bachelor pioneers named Toftezen, Sumner and Freund arrived by Indian Canoe to stake a claim in Oak Harbor. They came from Norway, Switzerland and New England respectively. Dispirited veterans of the California gold rush, they had heard about Whidbey in Olympia, from Sam Hancock.

These three fellows were instrumental in the early growth of Oak Harbor. Although they left no surviving progeny, the descendants of Freund's niece and nephews, whom he brought over from Switzerland, still live on the original Donation Claim.

Soon they were joined by the Wallaces at Crescent Harbor and the Irish Maylor Brothers on Maylor Point. The Maylor's extensive migration took them from Ireland through New York, to Panama, San Francisco and various points on Puget Sound. The Maylors left their mark and roots for several generations of descendants when they built a wharf and store at Maylor Point.

They were followed by more Irish immigrants who landed on Whidbey in 1858. The McCrohan family came via Australia with the Nunans and the O'Learys. The Nunans, McCrohans, Morse, Barrington and O'Leary families on northern Whidbey all descend from the boatload that landed there in 1858.

John Izett, a Scot ships carpenter settled at Crescent Harbor, where he worked as foreman at the Grennan-Cranney Mill in Utsalady for several years and in 1859 built Barrington's schooner, the *Growler*. He had learned his trade on the River Clyde in Scotland. He married Nancy Chenoweth, sister of the local judge. He built a cozy cabin, with a grand fireplace, furnished with furniture salvaged from a shipwreck that he had survived. He even rigged up a system of running water, using bored-out trees as pipes to bring spring water to the home. The next generation started a creamery that brought needed jobs to the community.

OTHER SOURCES OF INCOME

Although the main sources of income on the Islands were logging, farming and shipping, there was another less visible source of income: Smuggling! Whidbey Island's strategic location made it a natural port of call for the lucrative midnight trade, with the beaches of Mutiny Bay, Deception Pass and Smugglers Cove receiving much illicit cargo. Firearms, drugs and liquor, at one time or another, all entered the island this way. In the 1880's and 90's the cargo was often human: Chinese laborers.

The Chinese had been brought to America to build the railroads. When those jobs ran out, they became farm workers in various locales on the west coast. Soon they started to turn up as a part of the Island County work force. They were quiet and industrious, often performing work the whites wouldn't. Most often they were to be found tenant farming and clearing land. They were predominantly bachelors who came to work and send money home to China. Few had any intention of settling and in most cases were not permitted to own land.

Hobart Race remembered vividly the role of the Chinese his family hired to help plant and harvest potatoes. They also had their own plots and potato stocks which they marketed when the price was best.

They lived in a small "China House" on Race Lagoon until 1918. They were honest, moral and kind to the children, but they were never accepted as part of the community. Most were vainly struggling to buy passage back to China. Few ever did and they finally died out.

During the depression of 1893, racial problems erupted. The protesters complained that the Chinese exported most of their income, and replaced white men who needed jobs. Vigilante groups threatened violence; and in the climate of hard times their paranoia spread until an edict was declared for the removal of the Chinese.

Unfortunately, the Chinese were exploited as railroad workers, exploited as farm labor and the harassment they suffered at the hands of the Island townspeople just added insult to injury. Their role in Puget Sound, unfortunately, was similar to their position elsewhere in the young nation. They were ill-used and regarded as non-persons.

Chapter Five

WHIDBEY ISLAND SETTLEMENTS

SAN DE FUCA/COVELAND

The first settlement on Whidbey Island was in its central part, at Coveland, at the head of Penn Cove. It began as a port to ship out timbers and poles. The first trading post was established in 1853 on Barstow Point, where the Captain Whidbey Inn stands.

Coveland was the site of the Island's first sawmill, which was powered by waterwheel turned by the outgoing tide, the first post office, established in 1857, and the first County Courthouse, which still stands, a restored private residence, on the shore near Kennedy's Lagoon on Madrona Way. Soon there were two stores to serve what some say were as many as 800 people living in the area. Rapid growth brought the establishment of the first school in Island County.

Elsewhere, Donation Land Claims clustered around the ports of Oak Harbor and Coupeville laid the foundations for the next communities. "Far away" south, beyond the wilderness of forests and natives that the north islanders considered to be south Whidbey, outposts of individual claims were being established, but nothing resembling a white settlement.

The only regular link these pioneers had with the world, and with each other, was the mailboat. A turn of the century post-mistress, Sibella Barrington Fisher, wrote in her memoirs about the importance of that link:

"In the early pioneer days of Whidbey Island, about 1850, the only mail service was by sailing vessels on Puget Sound. The mail was left at Port Townsend where it was picked up and dispersed when convenient.

"A regular mailboat, the *Major Tompkins*, began landing here in the spring of 1858, bringing the mail to Ebey's Landing. The first postoffice was established in San de Fuca on June 4, 1890. The building was about 16 x 20 ft. It was situated in the heart of town about one block from the wharf. A few years later it was moved next door into the store.

"Henry C. Power was the first postmaster...The mail was brought to the wharf by stern wheeler. The *Fairhaven* carried passengers, freight, and the mail between Seattle, Whidbey Island and La Conner. After the *Fairhaven*, the propellers took over. Three steamer ships, *Camano*, *Whidbey* and *Calista* all served the little post office and provided transportation for early pioneers.

"The highlight of the day for the community, young and old, was to gather at the store and post office to gossip, buy groceries and wait for the mail to be distributed. Some would walk down to the dock to wait for the boat. Others watched from the store porch. It was always a thrilling sight to watch the boat come in. Some had walked a long distance carrying old-fashioned kerosene lantern in the wintertime. The day

Picture courtesy of the Puget Sound Maritime Historical Society

The sternwheeler Fairhaven *alongside a pier showing wooden plank construction. Passengers rode on the upper deck. The main deck was utilized for freight, fuel and engines.*

was just not complete without that evening trip to meet the mail boat."

Imagine standing on the dock, straining to see the first glimpse of the stern-wheeler steamer *Fairhaven* gliding through the channel between Whidbey and Camano, seeing the white puff of smoke coming from her stack, catching the sound of the whistle reaching across the water. Imagine the excitement of anticipating a letter with news from far away, a newspaper, or a package with fabric for a new dress. This boat and the mail were connections to the outside world in a time when there were no telephones, radios, televisions or any other kind of rapid communication. We sometimes forget it was their life line.

Near Coveland, loggers cleared the land, and farming was getting underway. Early agriculturists found rich soil in Ebey's Prairie, named for Col. Isaac Ebey. Together with Samuel Crockett and pioneer family's Engle and the Hill brothers they enriched and cultivated this soil and marveled to folks back east at it's production. Before long island timber and agricultural products found ready markets from San Francisco to British Columbia.

In the 1880's, with talk of a possible railroad the name of the settlement was changed to San de Fuca by a land syndicate. Visions of a great city rising here caused men to dream great dreams. The little community of San de fuca did "take off" for a while and promoters attracted new people to join residents of long-standing. The town that was platted had some real potential, with houses, a hotel, and shipping business established. Several professionals "hung out their shingles."

In 1893 a boatload of Dutch settlers arrived. They had heard of the outstanding productivity of the land from a Mr. Werkman, a remnant promoter of the land company that had attracted fruit growers to the Dugalla Bay area, who had gone to Michigan to attract new people.

These were welcome settlers, who brought operating capital, agricultural knowledge, industry and thrift, attributes needed to survive in difficult economic times. Eventually they attracted more friends from Holland and Michigan. By 1896 there were 200 Hollanders on north Whidbey. They farmed in San de Fuca, Swantown, Crescent Harbor and Clover Valley. They logged and began businesses in Oak Harbor. They and their descendants were to have great influence in the development of northern Whidbey.

COUPEVILLE

The Alexanders, Lovejoys and Coupes were the first to settle in Coupeville. They were joined by several other sea captains, who liked the all-weather anchorage close to the Utsalady sawmill. Soon there were several elaborate homes stocked with fine china and furniture, libraries, musical instruments and other amenities of culture. The townspeople formed churches, schools and community associations. They began to plan for the goods and services that settlers would need.

Known as the "City of Sea Captains", Coupeville was established in 1852 and is one of the oldest towns in the State of Washington. It is named for Captain George Coupe, the only man to sail a full-rigged ship through the waters of Deception Pass, who landed at the site of the future town and filed a 320 acre land claim.

Years before the town was platted, Captain Coupe gave one acre apiece of his claim to the Methodist Church and the school. The present day high school is still located on that parcel in Prairie Center. The town, the island's largest community, became the county seat in 1881.

Transportation between Whidbey and Camano Islands was established with a daily ferry from Utsalady by 1861. The big event of the day was when the daily boat arrived, bringing visitors, mail and products.

By 1884 Coupeville was praised as one of the most pleasant towns on the west coast. It had three hotels, a school, two taverns, a general store, drug store, a blacksmith and a wagon shop. It provided the kinds of services needed by Island settlers. The dressmaker was there, the drug store, and the Lovejoy Brothers Lumber company was always busy.

By 1890 Coupeville boasted wharves, warehouses and a real estate office. There were two churches and the Puget Sound Academy, attended by young men and women from all over the Sound. The community experienced a building boom. The 500-foot-long Coupeville Wharf served ships trading in wool, lumber, root crops, grain and apples. It was a popular moorage because large steamers could tie up, regardless of the tide.

The center of Island social life was in Coupeville. Residents produced amateur theatricals, the town band provided music and even a circus came to town in 1891. A gun club was established, a "magic lantern" was acquired and pictures shown. A baseball team was organized and in May, 1891, the steamer *Wildwood* brought a crowd of 200 to watch the game.

OAK HARBOR

Oak Harbor was named for the Garry Oaks that were so numerous that they extended clear to the water's edge in the 1850's. Development was slow. On arrival, a handful of Irish settlers found Skagit Indians almost the sole occupants. An amicable relationship was established and they co-existed in peace.

Other settlers that found their way to Oak Harbor were the Dutch and the Chinese The government had offered land at $1.25 an acre, but the railroad bought it up, holding it for eventual profit. When it was sold, it went to a land company who hoped to sell to fruit growers. This company scheme never worked, but it led to the eventual migration of Dutch farmers to the area.

The Hollanders were welcomed for their industriousness as well as their reputation for being well-to-do farmers. In

1889 Oak Harbor had 20 residents. Hardly more than a village, Oak Harbor's people were a happy, hard living bunch, who found time to sing, dance, race horses and laugh.

On the Fourth of July a celebration in Oak Tree Park brought people from Coupeville, La Conner and Utsalady by boat; others came by wagon and on horseback. Here settlers and natives gathered together for a picnic and clam bake, called a "mamook muckamuck" in Chinook jargon, meaning "work food."

There were canoe races, contests, and music. One year an artillery salute from Maylor's Wharf almost burned down the warehouse and dock. A piece of bunting had caught fire and set the shingles ablaze. Fortunately it was quickly extinguished and the long day ended with an all night dance.

In 1892 Oak Harbor experienced a mild boom. New people arrived and built homes and businesses, and a bank was established.

SOUTH WHIDBEY

Several logging operations were flourishing on the south end of Whidbey in 1851. The trader, Robert Bailey, had a trading post near the Digwadsh Tribal Village at Cultus Bay. He loved and respected the land and its people, and even married a Digwadsh woman. There was, also, a fish salting camp at Scatchet Head that operated from 1853-57, buying fish from the Indians. By 1859 Bailey was the Indian agent for several tribes totaling 1,600 people. His children married natives and the family's land and business prospered.

At the time Nathaniel Porter arrived to take over a claim at Mutiny Bay. He had gone to sea at age ten, sailed the world over, been a cavalryman, homesteaded in Port Ludlow, and had many other adventures before settling down on Whidbey Island at the age of 19, to raise crops and a family.

Near Double Bluff, William Johnson and his Snohomish bride, Jane, or Gah-toh-litsa, were farmers and had several children. Johnson rowed his produce, across rough, often treacherous, open water to Port Townsend. One night in 1886, when returning from Port Townsend he lost his life. His family believed he was robbed of the money he had made selling produce and murdered. His widow then married Edward Oliver, who was a logger at Deer Lagoon. Their combined family was numerous. Jane Johnson Oliver lived until 1945 and is still remembered as a colorful character.

Thomas John Johns, Oliver's partner, was so taken with Puget Sound that at 19, he jumped ship from the British Navy and homesteaded, with his wife, near Deer Lagoon.

Another sailor, a Portuguese, Joseph Brown, left his ship on Whidbey's east coast and integrated himself into the life of the native village at Sandy Point where he started a lighthouse. He married an Indian woman and they had 14 children. They began a school, and as other white settlers arrived, became leaders in that early community.

Some years later a dock, store and post office were established at Clinton by the Hinman brothers of Michigan. Because of the freshwater creek which flowed through the area, Edward Hinman began supplying fresh water for the steamers that plied the sound. The steamer traffic, also drew cord wood cutters, and the community was off to a great start.

And the little community of Keystone gained some notoriety as a sin city during the early days of Fort Casey, because of an infamous tavern located there, which was frequented by army personnel.

LANGLEY

The real town on south Whidbey was Langley, founded by Jacob Anthes, a German immigrant. At the age of 14 he had emigrated to New York and then come west on the first continental railway. He came from Seattle to Whidbey to hold a claim for someone and found the terrain and wildlife to his liking. Since he was too young to file for a homestead, he bought land, and brought other young men from Seattle to help him log and build a cabin.

In his spare time he explored the Island and determined the best site for a town. In 1889 he got the Langley Land Improvement Co. to help him incorporate a town. In the same year he married Leafy Weeks - by age 21 Anthes had accomplished much. He went on to effectively organize Langley by building a dock, hotel and store, and a road into the interior to encourage commerce .

EDUCATION

By the 1890's schools and social infrastructure were underway throughout Island County. Good education was purveyed at one room schools all over the Islands. Some sea captains did not find them up to their standards and took matters into their own hands.

According to George Kellogg's "History of Whidbey Island", "One captain wrote to friends in the east asking for help in getting school teachers who would conduct themselves with more dignity. He raised a protest against schoolmasters who slid down straw stacks with their pupils at the lunch hour and played kissing games with them in the evening. As a result of this letter, one young lady came west to teach, resolved to maintain the requisite decorum; which she did by promptly capitulating in a marriage with a dignitary of the school board...." The settlers supported the schools since there were no public funds available to sustain them.

TRAVEL

There were no public roads, although there were leanings in that direction by the 1880's. More settlers were coming to the south end, to Glendale, Maxwelton and Bayview areas. Before long roads were cut through that enabled horse or wagon to travel between Clinton, Langley and Useless Bay. There was little traffic with the north end of the Island, which was a sore point with residents of Langely who felt they were orphaned by the county government in Coupeville. Their only connection was the mailboat, or steamer, upon which the economy, personal travel and transport depended.

When the whole region suffered an economic slump, Whidbey farm products faced tough competition from California. Railroads were phasing out the steamers and indeed they would soon change the nature of travel and transport on the Sound.

RAILROADS

The coming of the railroads to the west coast influenced many aspects of life in Puget sound. Railroads changed everything and caused meteoric growth in Puget sound. Between 1877 and 1889 more people came here than in the previous 25 years. Even remote Whidbey Island was not immune to railroad fever. Hard as it is to believe, the mill town of Glendale, south of Clinton, had a railroad that ran from the saw mill to the dock.

There were land grabs by the Northern Pacific Railroad that made maritime jobs obsolete. In 1872 Jay Cook drew up plans for a rail terminus from the mainland to Holmes Harbor, or Penn Cove, touching off an explosion of land speculation. Two gentlemen from the Northern Pacific Railroad were observed in 1882 walking across a certain farm on Whidbey Island. They knocked on the farmers door and offered a price for the land that far exceeded its value.

A railroad was projected to run from Burlington, or Sedro Wooley across Saratoga Passage and over the Island to "New Chicago" around Admiralty Head. Speculators from Port Townsend planned a railroad ferry crossing to "New Chicago".

An Island County times headline in 1891 fueled the fire: "Come to Coupeville: A Railroad will traverse Whidbey Island within 12 months. Come and Settle before the rush."

There was speculation on the opportunities that railroad

access might bring. Men dreamt great dreams, even platting San de Fuca to become the terminus of a railroad, and lots were sold at high prices. The *San de Fucan* of 1890 printed a flurry of grand projections about the forthcoming "shipping headquarters of Puget Sound." There was talk of digging a canal across Ebey's prairie to give shorter access to the Strait of Juan de Fuca. Two villages, Chicago and Brooklyn, would flank the other end of the canal at today's Keystone ferry dock. A three-story hotel was even built at "Little Chicago" before reality and the depression set in, and the railroad scheme was off.

The high hopes for rail and canals perished, but the region continued to grow. Work was progressing towards a bridge at Deception Pass, commerce and building was happening in Oak Harbor. All over Island County people endured the slow time. The population grew and diversified and by the turn of the century there were several solid communities ready to embrace the future and the prosperity that returned with the Alaska Gold Rush.

THE UTSALADY SAWMILL AND THOMAS CRANNEY

For nearly 20 years , Utsalady (an Indian word meaning "Land of Berries") on the north end of Camano was an important place, with the feel of a bachelor's logging camp until the 1870's when a church, school, and other services needed by families were established. The Utsalady mill provided work for many Whidbey Islanders, processing logs from the mainland as well as from both islands.

Loggers felled and wrangled 12 foot diameter trees and skidded them out of the forest with teams of oxen. In 1867 the mill sent a 150-foot-tree to the Paris Exposition to serve as the United States flagpole and impressed the world with the magnificent timber from the Northwestern United States. Originally 200 ft.long, the pole had to be trimmed to fit on the ship that carried it.

One of the owners of the mill was Thomas Cranney, a Whidbey pioneer, who had sailed around the Horn from his home in New Brunswick, bound for the California gold mines. Eventually he landed on Whidbey where he opened a general store on Penn Cove. In 1855 he and his partners started the mill which operated until 1890.

Fine passenger ships were built at a Camano shipyard for the Northern Pacific Railroad. Utsalady was the port of registry for many vessels. Because there were no banks at the time, the town became an early financial hub, the deposit and distribution point for all moneys to that part of the sound. Sailors, loggers, pioneers, storekeepers and shipwrights collected their pay, or exchanged their cash here. Money came and went in $1,000 sacks of silver and gold.

Early in their partnership, a shipwreck at the mouth of the Columbia River nearly closed the mill, but Cranney and his partner picked up the pieces, got a loan and forged ahead, believing strongly in the need for and profitability of the sawmill. But in 1875, tragedy struck again, possibly the worst

The Acorn, *a small ferry that ran between Whidbey and Camano Islands. Although not of the period, it is an example of the inter island transportation that once existed.*

shipwreck off the Washington Coast, which would cause the mill's ultimate demise.

The steamer "Pacific" left Utsalady with the first shipment of grain from the Stanwood flats, $250,000 in gold from the mines, and 277 people aboard. Near Cape Flattery it collided with a sailing vessel and the Pacific sank immediately, losing all but two passengers. Cranney went on to serve many public offices on Whidbey, and with his wife Sarah Coupe, carried on an active social life. The mill continued under other ownership and gradually was moved to Port Gamble.

Eventually a ferry ran from Utsalady to North Whidbey until the early 20th century.

*Ships are but boards, sailors but men:
there be land-rats and water-rats,
water thieves and land thieves.*

The Merchant of Venice, Shakespeare

BEN URE ISLAND

A small, rocky island just inside Deception Pass, near Cornet Bay, was homesteaded by a canny Scot who named it for himself - "Ben Ure".

It became one of the wildest places on Whidbey Island, running opium, rum, and woolens. Ben Ure had tried farming, real estate, and raising cattle, to no avail. Finally he built a lighthouse, dance hall, and saloon on his island. Soon it became a place where loggers and tugboat men spent their time. Long suspected by revenue patrols of smuggling, he was always able to prevent the patrol boats from getting evidence. They were helpless, until one day when he was caught with contraband of cigars, whiskey, and opium, which led to formal charges. At his trial he told of smugglers he had helped, which included "Pirate Kelly," King of Puget Sound smugglers! When asked why it was that his Indian wife spent most of her nights on Strawberry Island, he said that she had a purpose: She would build a fire, and sit BEHIND it when the Revenue Patrol was around, and sit in FRONT of the fire when it was safe for the men to come through the pass to his island! What lonely nights she must have spent!

Ben Ure spent his last years on his island; today, few visit there, all the former clients of the saloon are long gone; Ben Ure had no children; and the lack of further facts give us the "Mystery of Ben Ure."

Picture courtesy of the Puget Sound Maritime Historical Society

The bark Hesper *differs from a square rigged, or full rigged ship because the after mast is rigged for a schooner sail.*

Glossary of Types of Ships, Boats and Rigs

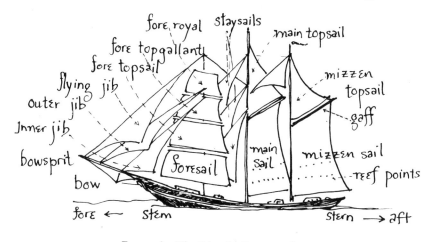

Example: *The Rig of a Barquentine*
a three masted vessel with only the fore mast square rigged,
main and mizzen mast carrying fore-and-aft mainsails and gaff topsails.

Brig: a two-masted square-rigged ship

Brigantine: a two-masted vessel square-rigged forward and schooner-rigged aft on the mainsail; also called a hermaphrodite brig.

Bark: a three-masted ship with foremast and mainmast square-rigged and mizzenmast fore-and-aft rigged. A four-masted bark has three front masts (foremast, mainmast, mizzenmast) square rigged and the fourth (jiggermast) fore-and-aft rigged.

Barkentine: a three-masted ship with foremast square-rigged, and mainmast and miz zenmast fore-and-aft rigged.

Clipper: a fast sailing ship, mostly built in Boston, or New York, it is a ship with long slender lines, an overhanging bow, tall raking masts, and a large sail area, sacrificing cargo space for speed.

Cutter: variation of single-masted sloop, with mast farther aft, almost halfway; always 2 headsails, called a forestay sail and a jib. Frequently has bowsprit to which jib is attached; headsails are smaller than on a sloop and easier to handle.

Downeaster: replaced the clippers in the 1860's and 70's after the gold dust had settled, when economy was again more important than speed; named after the State of Maine where they were built. They were more capacious than the clippers, built firm and stout, requiring half the crew and provided twice the payload of the clippers.

Fore-And-aft, or schooner rig: a sailing-ship rig in which most, or all of the sails are not attached to yards, but are bent to gaffs, or set on the masts, or on stays in a fore-and aft line (i.e.: length wise of the ship, from stem to stern).

Frigate: a square rigged war vessel intermediate between a corvette and a ship of the line.

Galliot: a long narrow light-draft Dutch or

Russian merchant sailing ship.

Packet: a passenger boat carrying mail and cargo on a regular schedule.

Rig: the distinctive shape, number and arrangement of sails and mast of a ship.

Schooner: a typically two masted (can be more), fore-and-aft rigged vessel with a fore mast and a mainmast stepped nearly amidships; a for-and-aft rig having two or more masts with the foremast of the same height, or shorter than the main mast; usually medium to large and of many designs. (i.e.. a three, four, or five masted schooner.

Ship, full-rigged: a square rigged sailing vessel having a bowsprit and three or more masts, each composed of a lower mast, a topmast, and a topgallant mast.

Sloop: a fore-and-aft rigged boat with one mast and a single head sail jib; the one mast is placed farther aft than in cat rig; carries a mainsail aft of the mast and a jib forward; mainsail may be rigged Marconi or (rare) gaff.

Steamer: a ship propelled by steam, initially generated by cordwood, later by coal or oil; a paddle wheel steamer, initially side wheelers, often using sail from Boston around the Horn to the West and North west Coasts; then using the engine for maneuverability and shore access.

Stern-wheelers were developed for inland waters and were particularly good in shallow waters near shore and in river rapids; finally in the 20th century paddle wheels gave way to propellers. .

Square rig: a sailing-ship rig in which the principal sails are extended on yards fastened to the masts horizontally and at their center.

Yawl: a fore-and-aft rigged sailboat carrying a mainsail and one or more jibs with a miz zenmast far aft.

Ketch and Yawl: both have two masts with main mast for ward and taller than the mizzenmast. Either may have one or more head sails (jib). Ketch mizzenmast is forward of rudderpost and not too short. Yawl miz zenmast is aft of rudder post and less then half as high as mainmast.

ship   Bark   Brigantine

Brig   Barquentine (BARKƎNTINƎ)   HERMAPHRODITE Brig

SCHOONER   Staysail schooner

47

Ships Common to Whidbey

Anadir
> Bark - Swift.

Burnhan
> Simeon Kinney sailed into Penn Cove.

Cabot
> Brig - sailed from San Francisco via Portland, to Penn's Cove.

Chalcedony
> Bark-H. B. Lovejoy and T. Kinney.

Calista
> Sailing Yacht Clapp boat charter member Coupeville Yacht Club.

Eclipse
> Schooner,31 feet - owned by Barrington and Phillips.

Franklin Adams
> Brig - Adams.

Growler
> Schooner- owned by Barrington, 62 ft long, 58 tons completed in1859. Built on Whidbey Island. Plied Puget Sound until 1868.

Jefferson Davis and **Joe Lane**
> Revenue cutters

Liteschi
> FreighterAdams

Lottie
> Schooner - Adams

Mariia
> Sloop 8.65 ton named for T. Coupe's daughter *Keturah* and *Mary Ellen* were built later named after two other daughters All three served the ferry route between PT. Townsend and Whidbey Island.

Mary Parker
> Schooner- Adams.

Onward
> Bark - S. Kinney.

Orbit
> Brig first ship owned outright on Puget Sound by a settler, Colonel Isaac N. Ebey. Purchased in 1850.

Shoo Fly
> Schooner- Kinney.

Success
> Bark that brought Capt. Thomas Coupe, half owner, to Puget Sound in 1852.

Success
> Steam boat named for Coupes other ship built at Utsalady 46 ft. long, beam 10 ft.

Tarquina
> Brig - Robertson - registered from Whidbey Island, built Perth Amboy, N.J. 1844, 90 ft long, beam 26 ft., depth 10 ft, 210 tons.

Willamette and Schooner
> Colonish" Brigs, owned by Thomas Coupe.

Note: These are ships picked from text that operated and were owned by folks on Whidbey. Probably incomplete.

Bailey Gatzert
built 1890 in Ballard.

Beaver
Steamer

Sternwheeler Skagit Chief, shows a low bow which was typical of Puget Sound Ship as there were no large waves to fear. This picture shows the use of cables, or steelrods, to help support the hull stresses and keep the boat from buckling.

"WHY SHIPS ARE SHES"

from collection of Stanley Lovejoy, author unknown

We always call a ship a "she",
    And not without a reason,
For she displays a well-shaped knee
    Regardless of the Season.
She scorns the man whose heart is faint
    And doesn't show him pity,
And, like a girl she needs the paint
    to keep her looking pretty.

For love she'll brave the ocean vast,
    Be she gig or cruiser,
But if you fail to tie her fast
    You're almost bound to lose her.
She's happiest beneath stars
    A time for speculation,
And has a hatred for all bars
    Just like a Carrie Nation.

On ships and dames we pin our hopes,
    We fondle them and dandle them,
And every man must know his ropes
    Or else he cannot handle them.
Be firm with her, and she'll behave
    When skies are dark above you,
And let her take a water-wave,
    And praise her, and she'll love you.

That's why a ship must have a mate;
    She needs a good provider;
A good strong arm to keep her straight
    To comfort her, and guide her.
For such she'll brave the roughest gales,
    And angry seas that crowd her,

And in a brand new suit of sails,
   No dame looks prouder.

A ship is like a dame at that;
   She's feminine and swanky;
You'll find the one that's broad and fat
   Is never mean or cranky.
Yes, ships are lady-like indeed,
   For take them all together,
The ones that show a lot of speed
   Can't stand the roughest weather.

The sternwheeler Telegraph was a sleek, streamlined ship, with a raked bow, designed to cut through the water at high speed.

Chapter Six

Red sky at sunset, sailors delight,
Red sky in the morning, sailors take warning.

THE SHIPS

The early ships that found their way to the shores of Whidbey, Camano and other islands of Island County came from far distant shores, captained by bold adventurers. Their ships were beautiful to behold with furling sails and sleek bodies They were like corks in the vast ocean sea, subject to the vagaries of the weather.

Today we send ships of another kind hurtling into space on voyages of discovery, with one major difference: they are in constant contact with the earth. There was no "mission control" to communicate with these early ships. They had few tools to chart their course. The art and science of navigation in those days on Puget Sound was often sorely tested. The masters of the tall ships came on the wind guided by a simple compass, a sextant, the stars and a strong sixth sense. There were no tide tables, no charts, no radar, no communication - they were often gone for months, or for years.

Still they valiantly set forth. First came the English, then the Spanish and others searching the world for other routes and lands. Even the Russians ventured down the west coast as far as Fort Ross in northern California before they retreated to Alaska. Jim Gibbs, in his book *West Coast Windjammers*, lists 546 commercial sailing vessels over 100 tons, constructed on the Pacific Coast from 1850 to 1908. Listed alphabetically by name, rig, tonnage, builder, place, date and ultimate fate, it is striking that most were wrecked, lost, foundered, stranded or sunk in collision, burned or blown up at sea. As many as sixty percent of the coastal schooners ended in one of the ways mentioned, taking a high toll of life.

Steamer runs, even short runs, were not without peril. Position in fog, or at night was estimated by timing the whistle's echo. At such tense times the captain lost his usual sociability and became very serious. Passengers would hear a short blast of the horn, then through the fog see the master lean out the door of the pilothouse, stopwatch in hand, to count the interval between the sound of the whistle and the returning echo. The technique has been referred to as Scandinavian radar and compared to an acrobat performing blindfolded on a high trapeze, without a net. Until the advent of lighthouses, warning buoys, charts, sophisticated navigational instruments and powerful engines, lack of visibility posed a constant threat. The timing the steamer's echo to determine the presence of land went beyond a mere mathematical estimate. It was based on the fact that sound travels through salt air at the rate of 1,080 feet per second. It was an art that brought home ships and saved lives.

Experienced navigators not only could estimate how far they were from the shore, but could determine their position by the sound of the echo. They took into account that a low coastline, a high bank, or a gravel beach all returned a different sound. The length of the echo was another factor. A short echo denoted a narrow island or headland as most of the whistle's sound passed on both sides. With only a few seconds leeway, the navigators also had to decide whether the echo was bouncing from floating logs, buoys or possibly a solid fog bank.

When, finally the time came for the settling of Island County the ships under sail that found their way to Penn's Cove, Utsalady and the channel between Port Townsend and Whidbey were varied and adapted to the type of work required.

The sea captains brought ships with them, as well as built ships here. Regular ferry service between Ebey's Landing, on Whidbey Island and Port Townsend was operated by Captain Thomas Coupe using a 27 foot sloop, built in Port Townsend. The *Marie* was named after Captain Thomas Coupe's daughter. Described as the first of its kind, she was built for speed and comfort, flying 150 yards of canvas, with a 36-foot mast, and 30-foot beam. She was built of the finest Northwest woods and even had a coach roof which could be opened on sunny days. Later Coupe had two other vessels built and named them after his daughters *Keturah* and *Mary Ellen*.

With the advent of the steamboat a regular schedule was established that operated much like a bus route. Leaving from Seattle the boats would stop at Edmonds, cross over to Whidbey Island stopping at Clinton, Langley, Freeland, Greenbank, Coupeville, San de Fuca, Oak Harbor and then on to La Conner.

The logs of sailing ships record many a trip from Whidbey Island to Portland, the Columbia River, Everett and Seattle. The Brig *Cabot* is well remembered historically as a ship that sailed from San Francisco via Portland to Penn's Cove.

The 1890's & 1900's were the glory days of the paddle wheelers and steamboats. They were elegant craft, usually offering staterooms, fine dining, cardrooms and other amenities for voyage around the Sound.

The Commerce, *a four masted schooner, showing how square sails were abandoned, allowing a smaller crew and providing more maneuverability.*

*T*he fair breeze blew, the white foam flew,
The furrows followed free;
We were the first that ever burst into the silent sea.

The Ancient Mariner, Part II, Stanza 5
Samuel Taylor Coleridge

THE TALL SHIPS

In the 1850's all significant transportation along the west coast moved by water. There was no other way. It must have been a beautiful sight to look across the water and see the many and varied ships working their way back and forth on the water "freeway."

The permanent white population of the future states of Washington and Oregon, known as the Oregon Territory, was almost non existent except for the occasional pioneer who ventured in to cut tall timber. Only Indians lived on Whidbey Island.

When the wild call of GOLD went out from California and was heard across the land, settlements on Puget Sound popped up like magic. They were always located with access to navigable waterways and to the great trees that grew down to the shore.

The tall ships that brought the early loggers and pioneer settlers to the Northwest and opened up Puget Sound to worldwide trade in lumber, coal and farm products, were square-rigged brigs, fore-and-aft rigged schooners, the mixed-rigged brigantines, barks and barkentines, and the smaller yawls, ketches and sloops.

The large clipper ships carried as much as two acres of canvas, based on the premise that the more sail the better, because of the need for speed. Developed by American ship builders during the 1830's and '40's and modeled after the smaller, swifter *Baltimore Clippers.*, these ships won maritime supremacy for the United States. This design eventually gave way to the Maine downeaster, designed to emphasize cargo space rather than speed, The schooner with fore-and-aft rigging replaced the square rigged ships. The fore-and- aft rigging was preferred because they were more maneuverable, with the strong economic advantage of reducing crews by half.

As the clipper ship *Windward* discovered in 1875 when it was stranded and helpless at Useless Bay off Whidbey Island, getting in and out of Puget Sound inlets was suited for these smaller more maneuverable craft. A medium sized clipper totaled 750 tons, and the giant of the clippers, *Great Republic*, was 4500 tons with a crew of over 100.

The dugout canoe, carved in one piece from a cedar log, was the village-to-village mode of travel before and after the coming of the white man because of its superior maneuverability.

One of the first small shipbuilding yards was located on Whidbey Island where Captain Thomas Coupe turned out several small schooners at a place that came to be known as Coupeville. By 1975, there were fourteen shipyards on Puget sound.

A SHIPWRECK

Under the icey waters of Puget Sound, an area of 1,721 square miles lie more than 600 vessels, victims of calamities that were often caused by human error. The most tragic shipwreck that occurred off the Washington Coast was the foundering of the steamer *Pacific* in the fall of 1875. She was outward bound from Utsalady when she collided in the dark south of Cape Flattery with the windjammer *Orpheus*. Cape Flattery at the northwest tip of the Olympic Peninsula is a magnet for bad weather and one of the many graveyards feared by captains and crew alike.

The *Pacific* struck the starboard side of the *Orpheus*, then bounded off, repeatedly striking the rigging, carrying away the backstays and bumpkin, and the main and main topsail braces, leaving the *Orpheus* in a wrecked condition on her starboard side. The wife of the *Orpheus'* captain came up on deck in her nightgown and was so infuriated by what she considered careless navigation on the part of the *Pacific* that she attempted to jump aboard the steamer. Her husband prevented her and the *Orpheus* sailed on into the night toward the Straits.

The crew of the Orpheus, occupied with unscrambling the damaged rigging, were unaware of the screams of the drowning from the Pacific behind them. The Orpheus proceeded to overrun the entrance to the Straits and piled up on Vancouver Island at Cape Beale. The ship was a total loss, but all hands escaped.

The *Pacific*, a wooden hulled sidewheeler, had 277 people aboard but only two survived, the rest drowning in spite of all emergency efforts of captain and crew. Corpses drifted up on coastal beaches for weeks.

NAVIGATION

The word navigation literally means getting from one place to another and having an idea of where you are along the way. Mariners who set out on voyages of discovery could not always know where they were, but with the help of a compass and a sextant they could guide their ships safely through unfamiliar waters.

The concept of the compass was discovered by the Chinese around 2,500 B.C. when they found that a certain piece of ore, floated on a piece of wood, would turn with one end pointed in the general direction of the sun at mid-day, which was south. It followed that the other end pointed north.

From this discovery came the compass needle, a strip of magnetized steel balanced on a pivot, free to swing in any direction. Left alone the needle always comes to rest with one end pointing north. The force that attracts the needle is the magnetism of the earth, which is like a huge magnet with one end in the north and other in the south. For a long time the compass housing was marked with 32 points on the mariner's compass. Then it was determined that a 360-degree, full circle could be used. Today's compass shows 360 directions, or bearings, but the 16 most commonly used traditional compass directions are known as the "Compass Rose."

The compass, together with the sextant, an instrument that measures the angular distance between any two points, such as the sun and the horizon, helped our early adventurers to find their way.

SHIPBUILDING

The labor-intensive job of building a sailing vessel in the 1870's went through many phases. Visualization in the form of a wooden half model was the beginning. The model is basic because it allows the builder to see if the shape of the hull will allow water to flow around it and to see how *she* will ride in the water.

The sternwheeler Fairhaven *under construction. Massive amounts of wood were used. A master shipbuilder needed to find just the right tree for each curved section to provide maximum strength. Workers sized the lumber, using adzes, forming each piece to fit.*

This model is the basis for developing precise drawings, carefully committing the gentle curves of the hull to paper. These curves are called the *lines*. The drawings are then enlarged, and full-sized wooden patterns for the ribs and timbers are cut.

Usually, in the spring before the thaw, teams of men would head for the woods to select the proper trees, offeriing strength and clarity, with just the right curves for each rib. It is important that this is done before the sap flows as "sap-wet wood" will warp and twist.

Next the backbone of the ship, the *keel*, the "focus of strength" is laid, running a hundred feet or more. It must be as straight as an arrow and built of large strong wood logs. Everything rises from the keel, which rests on wood support blocks.

Gradually each rib is fitted, individually, and the skeleton of the great ship takes shape, revealing the lines of the original model. The decking pieces, called *floors* are placed spanning the area between the ribs.

During the winter months *caulking* is prepared from hemp fiber bound with tar, preparatory for filling the chinks in the hull. The caulking is done after the outside planking is accomplished with great care, some are heated so they can be contoured to fit. The twisted hemp, called *oakum* is twisted and forced into the hull and deck seams with a caulking iron and mallet. Up to seven miles of oakum was often needed to make a vessel watertight. The hull was then painted with red lead paint and the deck coated with hot tar. The keel was sheathed with copper to protect the wood from worms.

By the time the vessel was ready for launching she would have an identifying name, but be far from sea worthy. She would slide into the water near the yard where she was built, often with the help of a smashed bottle of wine or rum.

Once the ship was launched the work on the interior living quarters was completed, the masts put in place, braced and rigged, ready to receive the thousands of square feet of sails which had been hand-crafted by skilled sailmakers. Ironmongers had been busy for weeks forging the necessary hardware to handle and hoist the sails. With the installation of pumps, anchors and other necessary equipment the vessel was ready to receive supplies for the first voyage and set sail.

The needs for thirty men for four years were then stored in the belly of the ship: 100 barrels each of salt beef and pork. 131 barrels of flour, 2000 gallons of molasses, 1119 pounds of coffee, 24,000 cigars, 39 pecks of salt, 172 pounds of nutmeg, 36 pounds ginger, 319 pounds of tea, 864 buttons, three dozen suspenders, and the traditional supply of rum.

Picture courtesy of the Puget Sound Maritime Historical Society

Sternwheeler George E. Starr, *a small side-wheeler with a walking beam engine. On the sternwheeler ship the pistons ran horizontally to a sliding arm which was connected to the middle paddle.*

THE STEAMERS

Picture courtesy of the Puget Sound Maritime Historical Society

The steamer Norwood *loading in port.*

Less awe-inspiring than the tall ships, but equally important to the commercial development of the area were the steamers, known to the sailors as "tea-kettles", "steam-kettles", or "stink-pots". In spite of the smoke, odor and noise they made, they possessed a distinct advantage over the nobler ships of sail. They were more maneuverable, less affected by the weather and unpredictable prevailing winds.

Steamboats came early to the scene around Puget Sound, but did not effectively supplant the sailing ship as the dominant commercial vehicle in and out of the Sound, until well after the beginning of this century.

The *Beaver* a diminutive paddleboat, constructed in England for the Hudson Bay company, launched the Pacific Northwest into the steamboat age in 1836. She came into being by order of the Hudson Bay Company Board of Directors, placed in 1834, to build a steamboat at the Green, Wigrams and Green Yard on the Thames. They did this against the advice of their Chief Factor MacLoughlin, who preferred canoes paddled by Indians. It was an attempt to bring the industrial revolution to the wilderness.

Tiny, at 100 feet, the *Beaver* had a 20-foot beam, displaced 109 tons and had a top speed of seven knots. She had durable hull fittings of oak, elm, teak and teredo-resistant greenheart, and was powered by two side-lever engines built by Boulton Watt, generating 35 horsepower. Launched in May 1835, she proceeded under sail out of Gravesend to Fort Vancouver on the Columbia River, in 225 days, with her 13 foot diameter paddles carried on deck.

She was quickly determined to be too under-powered for work on the Columbia River and was exiled by McLoughlin to Puget Sound where she served for over fifty years.

Concerning the gender of ships: In our country, as in Italy, the ship "she" is feminine even when the ship's name is masculine, or non-human. It is left to the poet to divine why

Picture courtesy of the Puget Sound Maritime Historical Society

The bridge of the Norwood *showing the crew in their working clothes. They don't look like the type who would fall for the "I forget my ticket" story. Note that the windows of the pilot house either drop down or can be removed for air, or better vision.*

we think of her as female. (See poem *Why ships are She's*) In gallant France a ship, "he" is masculine. In more scientific Germany it is neuter. Spain shows some confusion on sexual orientation of ships, using both feminine and masculine. In storied England, for whatever reason the ship is feminine, or neuter, and so the *Beaver* was often referred to as "it".

The *Ferry*, a sidewheeler, was Puget Sound's first American-owned steamer. She was registered in Olympia in 1853 and had the misfortune to blowup in 1867. The *Eliza Anderson*, a 140-foot, 280-ton Portland-built sidewheeler, arrived on Puget Sound in 1858. Her average speed of nine knots quickly earned her a reputation for slowness. It was said, "No steamer went slower or made money faster."

When faced with competition her Seattle owners cut fares to as low as 50 cents round-trip between ports. When competition withdrew, fares bounced back to $10 and $20, depending on the destination. This at a time when steamer fares from Portland to San Francisco were $5.

Freight charges on the *Eliza* were high. Cattle rode for $15 a head, sheep $2.50, all other freight for up to $10 a ton. She held the $35,000 a year mail contract as well. Everyone on Puget Sound knew her, had walked her decks while traveling, or had worked as a deckhand, or below decks. Later, to the joy of kids of all ages, the owners installed a steam calliope that played "Yankee Doodle" or "John Brown's Body", as the vessel aged.

In 1885 the *Eliza Anderson* became a media celebrity when she was seized by immigration officials at Port Townsend and charged with carrying contraband Chinese, some of whom ended up as tenant farmers growing potatoes and other vegetables on the prairies of Whidbey Island.

Joining the new "smoke puffers" arriving from Sacramento and Columbia River, were sternwheel steamers built along Puget Sound. The first was the *Julia* in 1860, built at Port Gamble. Her only claim to fame was that she lost her first challenge race with the old *Beaver* across the Gulf of Georgia and disappeared, in shame, to work in California, where the pace was slower.

The small local steamers had a shallow draft design with no keels which allowed them to navigate up shallow waters. Some were simply a floating shed riding on scow like-hulls. Laden with sacked grain, apples, berries, eggs, poultry, meats, and everything from boom chains to whiskey, these little steamers worked around the clock providing farm-to-market and back-to-the-farm service, steadily supplying the early settlements.

Steamers were first fueled by cordwood, then later by coal and ultimately by oil. But the old wood burners of those early days were not efficient. The *Beaver* devoured up to 40 cords of wood per 24 running hours. In order to travel a day, the *Beaver* was forced to halt for two days while a crew of Indians cut wood.

Jacob Anthes, one of the founders of Langley and operator of the general store, estimated that between 1891 and 1893 his wood sales to the little steamers averaged 35 cords a day,

Sternwheeler Casey, *shows a broad, flat bow designed to push up against the shore to transfer cargo and store excess cord wood. They often burned up to five cords of wood an hour.*

employing seven teams and 25 woodchoppers. Sternwheelers, which became the choice over sidewheelers on the Sound because of their maneuverability, often burned up to five cords of wood an hour.

About 1885 the Mosquito Fleet, an armada of small, slim, sharp-nosed, wooden-hulled steamers, their freight doors but a few feet above the waterline, plied the Sound's marine highways on round-trip runs of only a few hours between ports. They carried farmers, loggers, fishermen, businessmen and weekend crowds, along with mail, sometimes a piano, and always supplies for the milltowns and logging camps. Among their provisions were fresh milk and produce, flour and canned foods, Flower Girl chewing tobacco, Russian Salve, Snowflake Lard, Kennedy's Medical Discovery, hoarhound lozenges for the children, Noyo axes, blanket-lined canvas coats, dresses and hats and blankets; all the necessities of life that were sold in the general or company stores.

The milltown workers and their families found a short Sunday cruise on a steamer a welcome cure for endemic cabin fever. For twenty years the Mosquito Fleet, a disparaging

The steamer Virginia V, *a shallow-draft sternwheeler, the last of the Mosquito Fleet that once served the Puget Sound. She is still in service, but now carries sightseeing passengers on Puget Sound.*

term coined on the Mississippi River to describe shallow-draft sternwheelers drawing only 16 inches, carrying freight and passengers, was the lifeline of our inland sea, stopping at anything resembling a dock, wherever a dollar was to be made. The *Virginia V* the last of the Mosquito Fleet can still be seen around the Sound, carrying sightseeing passengers.

Oh Captain! my Captain! our fearful trip is done!
The ship has weathered every rack, the prize
we sought is won,
The port is near, the bells I hear, the people all exulting.

Oh Captain! My Captain! - Walt Whitman

"Nantuckets Girl's Song"
First verse of a ditty

I have made up my mind now to be a sailor's wife,

To have a purseful of money and a very easy life

For a clever sailor husband is so seldom at his home

That his wife can spend the dollars with a will that's all her own.

Then I'll haste to wed a sailor and send him off to sea,

For a life of independence, is the pleasant life for me.

Author unknown

A LOOK AT THE LIFE OF AN EARLY SEAMAN

Sailors standing on the rigging of an early tall ship.

History tells many tales of successful young men who went to sea in the day of sailing vessels and at an early age achieved success as master of their vessel and wealth from their adventures. This was not typical of the life of the nameless seaman who served as crew. These men labored under very harsh and difficult conditions.

They sailed for months to the bottom of the earth around Cape Horn, referred to by them as "Cape Stiff," a barren rocky headland were the Atlantic met the Pacific. The weather was always stormy, or foggy, or both. These sailors were not angels - they were a rough, tough lot, these men before the mast, often drunk, misfits and troublemakers. They were used to hardships, uneducated, underpaid, underfed and ill clothed. Their diet was salt pork, salt beef, hard tack, beans and if they were lucky potatoes. To the ships master and his officers they were the scum of the earth.

Once the harbor was cleared, the master had sole authority in a totalitarian world. He could perpetrate any injustice his conscience would allow without fear of punishment in this life. Many captains were firm but fair and God-fearing, others, were sadistic despots, the master of hell ships, backed up by bullies and firearms. Their voluntary crew the dregs, criminals on the lam, or the involuntary shanghaied from their home.

Formal complaints were consistently dismissed because the word of "scum" against the word of a gentleman was not believed. Yankee shipowners, especially during the rush for gold offered prizes to masters for faster passage, so the crews were driven by any means necessary to press on all canvas the ship could carry and use every breath of wind to full advantage. Is it any wonder that many jumped ship in San Francisco and other ports to join the gold rush.

Compared to early Phoenician law which protected seamen after the shipmaster's first strike for not obeying commands, these citizens of the civilized world could be kicked to death, mained for life, or made stupid by a head blow from a belaying pin, plus other agonies that ruined their lives. It wasn't until 1895 that public opinion was mobilized and changes began to happen.

These "packet rats" left few records except for their chanteys like this one called "Time to Leave Her" which turned their plight into a melodious dirge that they sang as they worked:

Oh, the work was hard and the wages low,

Leave her, Johnny, leave her!

We'll pack our bags and go below,

It's time for us to leave her!

Oh, the work was hard, the voyage was long,

The seas were high, the gales were strong,

The La Conner, *a screw, or proprellor driven steamboat with the same general construction as the steamwheelers.*

The food was bad and the ship was slow,
But now ashore again we'll go.
It was growl you may but go you must,
It mattered not whether you're last or first.
I thought I hears the old man say,
"Just one more pull and then belay."
The sails are furled, our work is done,
Leave her, Johnny, leave her!
And now on shore we'll have our fun,
It's time for us to leave her!

In port these seamen who were paid $7 or $8 a month faired even worse than on board ship. On the Barbary Coasts of San Francisco and Port Townsend, Tacoma and Seattle. waterfront businesses preyed on them notoriously. The seamen went like bees to honey to the saloons to drink, gamble, dance, sing, brawl and fornicate in these cesspools of crime. These "pleasure palaces" were set up to separate the men from their money and bounce them back aboard an outbound ship.

Saloons and flophouses along the Port Townsend Harbor, nicknamed the Portal of Whiskey, had special trap doors to drop drugged, slugged, or drunk seamen into the waiting rowboats to be taken to a waiting ship after a brief stay on shore, shanghaied again. One Port Townsend dentist offered bargain dental work to a sailor who would wake a few hours later with an ether headache on the deck of a hell ship. This abduction for pay netted some unfortunates with no knowledge of sail, no experience going aloft or climbing out on a yardarm, even men of the cloth were caught by accident.

With the advent of steamers, local crews worked in a much more humane world. A typical Mosquito Fleet steamer usually had a crew of less than ten, including the captain, mate, chief engineer and his assistant. Crew members enjoyed their work in spite of low pay for long hours, with little time off. There was respect rather than abuse and there was no involuntary servitude. Skippers and chief engineers were paid $100 per month, deckhands and oilers $40.

Crew of the sternwheeler Fairhaven, *probably taken in a studio since few ships were so fancy nor were the men so clean and well groomed.*

Chapter Seven

ABOUT THE SEA CAPTAINS

In the last half of the 1800's, sailing vessels and their crews ventured far and wide; many began their voyages in eastern Canada and New England. With the exception of William Robertson, who was born in Virginia, they all came from New England or the Maritime Provinces of Canada. All were very young when they first went to sea and quickly rose in rank as leaders. The youngest, Thomas Coupe, was only 12 years old when he left home to follow a life of adventure on the sea.

They sailed from the Atlantic to the Pacific, around *Cape Horn*, a long, tedious and dangerous passage. Once on the western side of the continent they fanned out to the far East and to the north, looking for rich cargo.

Our Island County sea captains ventured here from a variety of other ports of call. They came north seeking gold and the rich harvest of the forest. When the time came for the Island of Whidbey to be settled the seekers found a jewel in the middle of Puget Sound, a land rich in timber and teaming with fish and wildlife, an island blessed with deep harbors, sweeping prairies and a fertile ground.

Here they found a land very similar in geography to their eastern homes, with the added amenities of majestic mountains and a mild climate. Fourteen sea captains decided to establish homes, marry and raise families here. Once their sailing days were over they became farmers, ship builders, store keepers and shapers of Washington State government.

A special thanks must be given to their wives and daughters who were the chroniclers, and who left diaries describing life in the early days. These women described a life that was often harsh, filled with the perils of the unknown, but at the same time fulfilling. Each of these pioneering people laid the foundation for life as we know it on Whidbey Island.

Death was a companion, childbirth a travail, survival was sometimes daunting but these early islanders maintained in a time when the "necessities" of today were unknown.

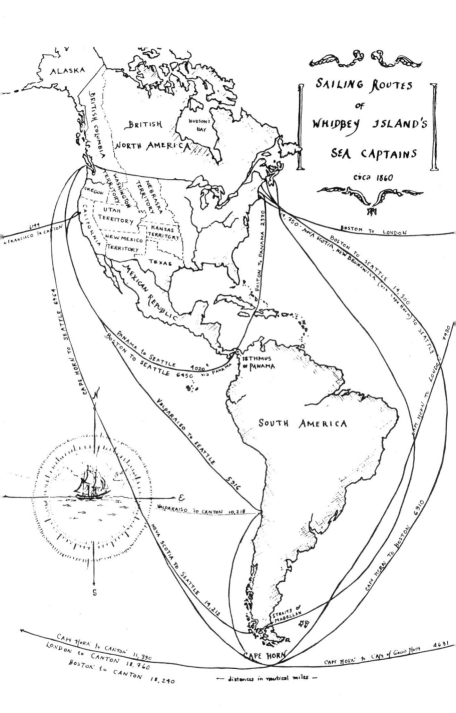

SAILING ROUTES
of
WHIDBEY ISLAND'S
SEA CAPTAINS

circa 1860

ALASKA

BRITISH COLUMBIA

BRITISH
NORTH AMERICA

HUDSON'S
BAY

WASHINGTON TERRITORY

OREGON

NEBRASKA TERRITORY

CALIFORNIA

UTAH
TERRITORY

KANSAS
TERRITORY

NEW MEXICO
TERRITORY

TEXAS

MEXICAN REPUBLIC

ISTHMUS
of PANAMA

SOUTH AMERICA

STRAITS of
MAGELLAN

CAPE HORN

S. FRANCISCO to CANTON 6199

BOSTON to LONDON

BOSTON to SEATTLE 14,300

NOVA SCOTIA, NEW BRUNSWICK (via CAPE HORN) to SEATTLE 750

BOSTON to PANAMA 2370

CAPE HORN to SEATTLE 6964

PANAMA to SEATTLE 4020

BOSTON to SEATTLE 6450 via PANAMA

VALPARAISO to SEATTLE 5516

VALPARAISO to CANTON 10,218

NOVA SCOTIA to SEATTLE 14,212

CAPE HORN to BOSTON 6910

CAPE HORN to LONDON 7380

CAPE HORN to CANTON 11,330

LONDON to CANTON 18,760

BOSTON to CANTON 18,240

CAPE HORN to CAPE of GOOD HOPE 4631

— distances in nautical miles —

N

E

S

Captain Jonathon Pierce Adams
Boothbay, Maine
1830 – 1902

Picture courtesy of Island County Historical Society

Born with sailing blood in his veins, Jonathan Adams grew up breathing the salty air and learning the ropes from his father, Captain John Adams. While young Jonathan had to attend Academy during the winters, each summer found him aboard his father's ship bound again for England, France, or Spain.

By the time gold was discovered in California, Jonathan was ready to cast off on his own as mate on a ship bound around the Horn. When the ship arrived in San Francisco in 1849, however, Jonathan caught gold rush fever, left his ship, and joined 80,000 others hoping for a strike in the California Gold Rush. Spurred on by initial good fortune, he headed north in 1852 to try his luck in the new Fraser River gold strike. This proved less profitable. After a short stay in Steilacoom, he invested his winnings in a hotel in Olympia and had a go at the life of innkeeper.

But his salty blood stirred, and the land couldn't hold him. He sold his hotel to purchase the freighter *Liteschi*. With the *Liteschi* and the brig *Franklin Adams*, which he managed, he busied himself shuttling freight around the sound, and down to Portland and San Francisco for most of a decade.

Then in 1862, gold fever seized him again. He gambled on the Cariboo mines of British Columbia, apparently with some success, for he was able to build the schooner *Lottie* and settle in for another ten years of sailing in trade on the sound.

In 1872 he built a final schooner, *Mary Parker*, which carried freight, including iron ore, cattle, hay, and grain, to all ports around the sound and Vancouver Island. In addition, the *Mary Parker* made a number of runs to the Arctic to collect seal oil. Records show that on some trips she carried 24 canoes and 48 Native Americans – they must have been given the dangerous job of capturing the seals. Eventually, with the advent of steam ships, Adams sold the *Mary Parker* to Native Americans, who hired two caucasian men to operate her.

At the age of 48, Captain Adams married. He had met his wife, Elsbeth Freund, while visiting the Eisenbeis family in Port Townsend. Elsbeth was a niece of Ulrich Freund, one of the three original settlers of Oak Harbor.

Elsbeth and her brother Arnold had traveled together from Switzerland to the East Coast, a trip that was miserably typical of travel at that time. Although they had purchased second-class tickets, somehow they were assigned to steerage. Arnold was ill the entire journey. After a rough train trip from Philadelphia to San Francisco, a kindly German hotel keeper took them in. This allowed Arnold time to recuperate while they tried to learn where Oak Harbor was located. Finally they heard that it was located near the Cariboo Mines in British Columbia. With this information, they booked passage to Victoria. Fortunately, Ulrich Freund thought to ask a neighbor who was traveling to Victoria to be on the lookout for his niece and nephew. When the neighbor found the two in a hotel, he brought them back to Oak Harbor in a small boat. Arnold was apparently so ill from this trip that he had to be carried ashore on arrival.

After staying a while with her uncle, Elsbeth found employment with the Eisenbeis family in Port Townsend. The family spoke only German but Elsbeth was determined to learn the language of her new country, which she did by studying the schoolbooks of the Eisenbeis children. Apparently she learned enough to charm Captain Adams, as well as to understand his marriage proposal.

With Captain Edward Barrington and his wife as members of the wedding party, Captain Adams and Elsbeth were married in style at the State Hotel in Coupeville. They set up housekeeping in Coupeville, where their first three children were born.

Then Adams, ready to retire from the hard life of a sea Captain, sold the *Mary Parker* and moved the family to Port Townsend where he built a large store adjoining his home. Two more children were born there. By 1896 they retired completely and the store was sold. They moved back to Whidbey Island to live on the Freund Donation Claim in Oak Harbor which had been divided between Elsbeth and her half-brother.

Although Adams's years in Puget Sound seem to lack the adventurous excitement of his youthful voyages and gold rush years, Adams was a vital part of the settlements and commerce of these new territories. Certainly he and his ships experienced many dangers among the treacherous tides, gales, and obscuring fogs of Puget Sound.

One dramatic rescue in Puget Sound is credited to Captain Adams. Emma Lovejoy Dyer and her two daughters had crossed Patridge Bank to spend a day with her husband Charles, a keeper of the Smith Island Lighthouse. Calista Lovejoy and her three children joined them for a lovely day's outing. As Dyer was sailing them back home in the small lighthouse boat, a sudden fierce squall blew in through the straits. Their little boat was in imminent danger of swamping when Captain Adams sighted the crew in distress, made a tack, and pulled them all aboard his ship.

It was initially feared that Mrs. Dyer might not survive. But after wet clothing was removed, Mrs. Dyer and the others were wrapped in warm blankets and given hot drinks, and all recovered completely.

Captain Edward J. Barrington
Nova Scotia
1818 – 1883

Picture courtesy of Island County Historical Society

The lure of the sea called Edward Joseph Carter Barrington from his native Nova Scotia at the age of fourteen years. By nineteen he was already the master of a vessel hauling water from Sausalito to the the new metropolis of San Francisco. Hearing of an urgent demand for pilings for the construction of wharves on San Francisco Bay, Barrington and a partner entered into a deal to sail north for a cargo of timber. Unfortunately, Barrington's first business deal turned sour when his partner absconded with the money.

In 1851 Captain Barrington signed a contract to carry mail from Olympia to Whatcom (now Bellingham) by dugout canoe. Several years passed, during which Captain Barrington developed a shrewd business sense. He took on a new partner, Charles C. Phillips, and together they bought the 31 foot schooner *Eclipse*, built in Port Ludlow. They got it at the bargain price of $600, but Barrington hit on an idea for a no-risk way to finance his portion of the schooner. He sent word to the Native Americans of the Skagit River area that he would pay one dollar a barrel for all the potatoes they would bring to the boat. Barrington made enough profit on the resale of the potatoes in San Francisco to pay for the vessel in one trip.

Ready to begin a new enterprise, he ran an ad in the Olympia newspaper stating: "Regular packet, not entirely dependent on the wind, the fast sailing schooner Eclipse, Capt. Edward Barrington, Master, will make regular trips between Oak Harbor, Penn Cove and Olympia, touching at intermediate places. For freight or passage." The new shipping business was launched successfully, sometimes making crossings to Victoria as well.

Soon the two partners were brewing up other schemes. They opened the first general store in Oak Harbor, where they had both settled, and had the goods delivered by boat. Next, they purchased two claims, the Sumner and Taftezon in the future townsite of Oak Harbor, thus gaining control of most of the waterfront. The main street of town was appropriately named Barrington Avenue – which it remained until the Navy came to Whidbey Island and changed the name to Pioneer Way.

Whether it was convenience, or an early publicity stunt, no one knows, but, Barrington and Phillips constructed a large boat on the beach next to their store. They hired their neighbor John M. Izett and three helpers to do the work. Nearby oak timbers were cut and sawed into planks. Felling and working hardwood timbers through a hard winter, the four builders did so much complaining that Captain Barrington named his new schooner *The Growler*. The ship, 62 feet long and registering 58 tons, was completed in 1859. The *Eclipse* was sold at once. A year later Barrington bought out his partner's share in *The Growler*.

Carrying flour, livestock, wheat, and general freight, *The Growler* plied the Sound until 1868. Captain Barrington sailed her to Sitka, Alaska, twice, and then sold her to Captain Ed

Lynch of Fort Wrangell. Tragically, on Captain Lynch's initial voyage out of Victoria, *The Growler* capsized off Cape Murray in the Queen Charlotte Islands. Many wondered if *The Growler* simply refused to go on without her original architect and Master, thus denying any others her service. She took down with her a $35,000 cargo from the American Fur Company. Four bodies and a small amount of wreckage and cargo were found by the natives, but the remaining twelve members of the crew and passengers were never found.

Captain Barrington now turned his attention to life on shore. Three years earlier, in 1865, at the age of forty-seven, he had married nineteen-year-old Irish coleen, Christina McCrohan. Christina's parents had migrated first to Australia, then were headed for the California Gold Rush when they were enticed by rumors of an island named Whidbey with similar landscape, coastline, and weather to the Ireland they dearly missed. Instead of stopping in San Francisco, they continued on to Port Townsend and from there on to San de Fuca. The land where the McCrohan's settled north of Point Partridge still shelters several of their fifth, sixth, and seventh generation descendants.

In an 1865 letter to his brother and sister, Barrington well describes his living and circumstance:

"I was married on the 13th of September to a Miss Christina McCrohan, with whom I am now living very comfortably in my house at Oak Harbor. My Partner, Charles Phillips, and myself own twelve hundred acres of good land here, reasonably well stocked, and furnished with the necessary barns, etc. We have two store houses on the beach, a store and warehouse in Coupeville, some six miles from here, across the Bay. Hay brings a fair price, cattle and hogs always do, so that on the whole, we get along pretty well. Sometimes we have good luck in our merchandising operations – again bad. . . again we own a schooner of sixty tons burden with which we occasionally do pretty well."

. . ." I have had on the whole a pretty hard life of it here, running about on small vessels, sometimes on government employment, sometimes on my own account – constantly speculating, sometimes successful and again losing nearly all I had made."

During their life together, Captain Barrington and Christina had six children, five boys and one girl. They also raised Barrington's daughter, Olivia, from a first "marriage" to a Native American woman. Such native "wives" were common among the settlers. Common, too, was their sad fate once the men contracted official marriages. But Christina, the official wife of Captain Barrington, being well-liked and applying herself to community service, became known as "The First Lady of Whidbey Island."

Lured by politics, Captain Barrington served one term in the Territorial Legislative Council as joint councilman for Island, Whatcom, and Snohomish counties. He resigned before the second session to tend to business matters. While dabbling in the lumbering business, he helped found the town he somewhat immodestly named Barrington. However a slip-up in recording the name in Olympia left the new settlement known as Darrington.

Not only was Captain Barrington a shrewd business man, but he was also a colorful rogue inclined to unorthodox humor, a measure of courage, and a streak of temper perhaps connected to his fiery-red hair. The natives, who both feared and respected his authority, called him "Sykes" (or "Sikes"), generally interpreted as "devil."

In many a fracas between Native Americans, he was considered both judge and jury. The native women would run to the Barrington home for the Captain's help when their men began fighting after drinking too much alcohol. He often settled the matter with a cane. His justice was swift, if not always well-considered. One incident serves to illustrate Barrington's legendary temper: "Big Billy," a Native American who stood 6 feet tall, decided to test Barrington's authority while helping him butcher on a bank above the bay. When asked to "Hand me that gam-stick," Big Billy retorted that he had decided to be boss now. Barrington grabbed the gam-stick, knocked Billy down with a blow, seized him by the hair, and heaved him over the bank. The settler helping Barrington with the butchering protested that he was afraid Barrington had killed Big Billy, to which Barrington replied, "That was the intention." Four days later a very subdued Big Billy appeared before the Captain saying, "You still boss."

On the other hand, his personal intervention saved many a native from violent death at the hands of other settlers. The Native Americans also considered the caucasians a sort of insurance against the brutality of the Haidas who would carry slaves back with them to Vancouver. One day a frightened native girl ran screaming to the Captain that a raiding party of the Haidas had been spotted. Barrington made his plans as he ran, arriving at the camp just as the painted Haidas landed. He stood bravely in front of the raiders, counting on his size and flaming hair to shock them, giving himself a momentary advantage. Then he horrified both the attackers and their intended victims by cutting the thongs that held an ancient burial canoe, scattering the bones on the ground. Without a pause, Barrington hoisted the skull on a long stick and began a slow, ritualistic dance parading the skull up, down, and around before the transfixed natives. So horrified were they at this desecration of their spirit world, they forgot the spears at their sides. With a final blood-curdling yell, Barrington leapt at the Haidas, and they scrambled chaotically to their canoes, screaming, "Memaloose! Memaloose!" (Evil spirit) and "Sike! Sike." The redhaired Irishman reportedly shook with laughter before the stunned band of Skagits. Thus came the end of Haida raids into Oak Harbor and the cementing of Barrington's reputation as a true devil who dared enter the sacred, forbidden world of the dead.

Ironically, this robust man spent his latter years partially paralyzed. He died at his residence in Oak Harbor at the age of 64. Captin Barrington's and Christina's daughter, Sibella, married Christian Fisher, and they built and ran the popular Glenwood Hotel in Coupeville, which was located on the present site of the Island County Historical Society Museum.

The hotel was destroyed by fire in 1969. Four of his five sons who evidently inherited their father's "fighting Irish" temperament, became sea captains notorious in the Yukon during the Klondike Gold Rush.

*H*ow dear to my heart are the scenes of my childhood,
     When fond recollection presents them to view!
The orchards, the meadow, the deep-tangled wildwood,
     And every loved spot which my infancy knew;
The wide spreading pond, and the mill that stood by it;
     The bridge and the rock where the cataract fell;
The cot of my father, the dairy house nigh it;
     And e'en the rude bucket which hung in the well!
The old oaken bucket, the iron-bound bucket,
     The moss-covered bucket which hung in the well.

The Old Oaken Bucket, from the song - Samuel Woodworth

Captain Joseph Warren Clapp
Scituate, Massachusetts
1843 – 1940

Picture courtesy of Island County Historical Society

In May 1843, on the farm that inspired the song "The Old Oaken Bucket,"(a song written during Revolutionary War days by Samuel Woodworth, composer) Joseph Warren Clapp was born. Like Captain Holbrook, he could trace his ancestry back to the Mayflower pilgrim Richard Warren.

But by the age of 19, Joseph Clapp decided to leave that farm and make the ways of the sea-faring man his career. And for the next 27 years, he sailed around the Horn many times and made several trips to China. He initially worked out of Atlantic coast ports, gradually rising in position until he became second mate of the full rigged ship *Tecumseh*.

In 1879, in his 36th year, he migrated to the Pacific coast and for five years was master on the bark *General Butler* owned by the powerful Puget Mill Company. He also served as master of the *Atalanta, Jabey Howes*, and the *Charmer*, a 1,885 ton wooden bark which launched out of Bath, Maine in 1881.

One of Clapp's surviving sea stories has him plucking a cask of brandy, covered with barnacles, from the southern Pacific Ocean. The rocking action from years of drifting on the sea had a refining effect on the brandy, making it very valuable. Because of this unique aging process, Clapp was able to sell the brandy in Melbourne for a fancy price.

Clapp had remained a bachelor for 43 years – until he made a trip to Puget Sound. Here the dashing, handle-bar mustached Captain Clapp met, courted, and married the beautiful, brown-eyed Mary A. Cranney, better known as Miss Mollie. Three years later he "swallowed the anchor" and settled in Coupeville where he and Mollie lived for the next half century.

In the 1890s, Clapp's sailing adventures were restricted to the *Calista*. This *Calista* is not to be confused with the steamer *Calista*. This was a racing yacht carrying 240 yards of canvas. Built on Whidbey Island, captained by Clapp, and owned by his partners H.B. Lovejoy and Ben Lovejoy, the *Calista* made her maiden voyage to Bellingham Bay on July 1, 1894 and was a charter member of the Yacht Club organized the next year in Coupeville.

Having no children to otherwise occupy them, Captain Clapp and the charming, elegant, and sociable Miss Mollie became active members of the community. Miss Mollie, a native of Coupeville, kept the house and herself always dressed up and ready for visitors. Once a month, on Visiting Day, she put on her gloves, took her visiting cards and made her social visits.

In the gay 90's, Coupeville was the center of social life on Whidbey Island. There were two dominant factions: the Methodists, who confined their social zeal to church functions; and the Congregationalists, who believed in plays and dances. Hosting whist, bridge card games, and other social gatherings in their home, Clapp and Miss Mollie were considered to be a part of the liberal faction.

In 1890 the Methodists and the Congregationalists declared war over sermons printed in the *Island County Sun* which expressed liberal tendencies. This mobilized the Methodists to join forces with a conservative real estate firm and, of all things, the town saloon keeper, to close down the paper. Captain Clapp and others took a strong stand and prevented this from happening. The fundamentalists, in retribution, were able to start a rival newspaper, the *Island County Times,* in which "unseemly personalities and vulgar vituperations have no place." This led to serious word battles being waged in the press.

In spite of the controversy and still a respected and vital part of the community, Clapp was selected with others to recommend a permanent location for the seat of government for the island county, locating it in Coupeville. Over the years he served his community as Deputy County Clerk, Deputy County Treasurer, Justice of the Peace, and from 1898 to 1915 Clapp served as the Coupeville postmaster.

All of his life Clapp took an active part in the Masonic Lodge, serving as Worshipful Master for four consecutive years beginning in 1897. Eventually he became Senior Past Master of Washington Masonry and served seventy years as a Master Mason, Whidbey Island Lodge No. 15. In celebration of his tenure, a celebration banquet was given in his honor.

Those who remembered Captain Clapp in his later years recall a prankster with a hearty, infectious laugh who loved children and was full of fun. In his home was a bay window and nearby was a table where he kept models of two ships he had commanded. As an old man, he would sit there smoking his pipe and gazing out over Penn Cove.

Clapp died at his home in Coupeville March 31, 1940, seven weeks before his 97th birthday. Ironically, final rites were held at the Methodist Congregational Church. The obituary in the *Island County Times* would have given him great pleasure because the paper that opposed his side in the dispute between the Methodists and the Congregationalists stated:

"With his passing has gone one of the finest mentalities this community has known – a man well read and with a remarkable memory. . . The Captain was a man of dignity, jovial and merry, with a happy laugh – a splendid type of Old New England gentleman, sturdy, honorable and reliable. . . These last lines from a tribute paid him on his 95th birthday seem fitting: 'Dear Captain, We wish you fair gales, Good Tides, and the sun on your sails."

Miss Mollie died the next year.

Captain Thomas Coupe
Nova Scotia
1818 – 1875

Picture courtesy of Island County Historical Society

As a young boy, Thomas Coupe probably spent many a night in Nova Scotia listening wide-eyed to sea tales in his father's inn – stories of sea monsters, storms of legendary proportions, and sea captains stringing disobedient seamen from yardarms. Apparently intrigued by these tales, rather than frightened, young Coupe was off to sea with the merchant marines by the age of twelve.

On the other hand, perhaps young Tom was simply escaping a crowded home. He was Thomas and Mary Coupe's firstborn, but his mother had brought seven children from a previous marriage. By the time young Tom was six, he had ten brothers and sisters.

Whatever his motivations, Tom became an experienced seaman. His travels had taken him back and forth to England and down to Maine. In Wiscasset, Maine, he succumbed to the charms of Mary White, and they were married in 1840 when Coupe was twenty-two. They settled in Brooklyn, New York, where five children were born over the next ten years; the youngest, Emma, lived only ten weeks.

By the time gold was discovered in California, Thomas was seasoned and ready to engage the adventure. Commanding the schooner *Rochester*, Captain Coupe headed for California – along with 725 other ships packed with 30,000 passengers. Coupe's journey by ship to the gold fields was the stuff of legends – tales to rival any he'd heard at his father's inn.

The trip from Boston to San Francisco took 125 days in a schooner, bark, or brig. One of the most awesome natural obstacles of the trip were the Straits of Magellan on the tip of South America. "No scene," wrote one traveler, "is more calculated to fill the beholder with awe and a sense of the impotence of Man." The passage through the straits was 300 miles long and only a mile and a half wide at its narrowest point. But young Captain Coupe sailed safely through and on to San Francisco.

Once in California, Captain Coupe must have been tempted to try his luck in the gold fields. Thomas Coupe, however, set his sights on a more certain "gold." Logs were desperately needed for wharves in San Francisco harbor and for the newly drilled mine shafts. Northern California had trees, but they weren't easily accessible. But the trees in the Oregon Territory grew right down to the water's edge. Even though a round trip to Whidbey Island took about two months, it was cheaper to ship logs than drag them over land. Thus, Douglas Fir (or Oregon Pine, as it was first called) became Washington's – and Coupe's – "gold."

Captain Thomas Coupe acquired part ownership of the bark *Success* and went to work hauling logs from Utsalady on Camano Island to San Francisco. It was during one of these trips, running behind schedule for a load of pilings, that Captain Coupe took a short cut through Deception Pass. He must have known that the tide rips through the narrow channel at seven knots. It may have been expediency – or an exciting challenge to a young captain with twenty years at sea under his belt. He was notorious for carrying all sail, at all times, under all conditions, and pushed the 14-knot limit of his vessel many a time – a gambler at heart. This notoriety and his earlier experience sailing through the Straits of Magellan must have emboldened him enough to become the first person to sail a full-rigged ship through Deception Pass – a true measure of Coupe's courage and skill.

There is no record of what the fifteen to twenty man crew thought of their daring captain, but the penalty for disobeying a sea captain was severe. On later trips, they were bound for San Francisco under as much sail as the ship could carry, hoping to improve time to San Francisco. When a storm blew up, Coupe, as usual, stubbornly insisted on keeping all sails aloft. Only when the storm reached such intensity that it threatened to capsize the ship did Coupe capitulate and give the order to reef sail (take sail down). This time the crew refused. It must have been a formidable, gale force storm for the crew to fear climbing the mast to reef sail more than they feared the Captain's certain punishment. Not willing to lose ship, crew, and load, Coupe climbed the mast himself and reefed the sail. He claimed later that the wind was so strong that his new pair of tough canvas, bell bottom britches caught a gust of wind up the leg and ripped to shreds. There is no record of what penalty, if any, was meted out to the crew.

Though still sea-bound, Coupe didn't entirely escape gold fever. In 1852 Captain Coupe and his new partner, J.H. Van Bokkelin, arrived in the *Tepic* to find that gold had been discovered on Queen Charlotte Island. In B.C. Captain and crew spent several days bartering knives, arms, and fishhooks for furs and gold dust. Van Bokkelin and Coupe had managed to secure about $800 in gold before the natives caught on to the fishhooks-for-gold scam. Captain and crew made a hasty exit.

It was while loading logs from Utsalady, sometime in late 1851 or early 1852, that Captain Coupe took a longboat and visited Penn's Cove. The island must have appeared a nearly uninhabited version of his boyhood haunts in Sidney, Nova

Scotia. He immediately staked a Donation Land Claim of 320 acres bordered by John Alexander on the west, John Crockett on the south, and by Penn's Cove to the north.

Coupe had found a home – and what is home without a family? So he sent for Maria and the four children. They boarded the *Thomas Church* for the six month trip, a journey which gave four-year-old George his first taste of the sea. Captain Coupe met the family in San Francisco and brought them on to Whidbey Island in 1853, the same year Washington was organized into a territory.

Upon arrival, Coupe was stunned to find that his staked, but unrecorded, claim was occupied and filed on by C.H. Ivans. Coupe was able to convince the man that his was the prior claim – or was it the $100 to vacate that did the convincing? Whatever the deciding factor, speculation indicates that had the Captain been less convincing, the fledgling town might have been called Ivansville.

In the log cabin where the Coupes lived during their first year on the Island, a fifth child was born. The Captain had contracted with Nathaniel Hill to build a house in Coupeville, and shortly after moving in, the last of the Coupe children was born. Built with redwood boards from San Francisco, their home was the first frame house built in Coupeville and still stands on Front Street.

About this time, influenced by several factors, Captain Coupe began centering his shipping around the local trade. As gold veins petered out, the California ports experienced depression. And more immediate motivation to stay closer to the family came from the tension which had begun to escalate between the new settlers and the island natives.

Small block houses were being erected here and there should fighting erupt. For further protection, the revenue cutter *Jefferson Davis* arrived on the sound in 1854 under the command of Captain Pease. Captain Coupe's expertise was called upon to pilot the *Jefferson Davis*, as well as the *Joe Lane*, another cutter sent in at the height of the conflict in late 1859 and early 1860.

When he wasn't busy on the revenue cutters, Coupe ran freight to Victoria, B.C., as captain of the brig *Willimantic* and the schooner *Colonish*, both owned by W.T. Sayward of Port Ludlow. By the end of 1859, Thomas Coupe was making plans to secure the ferry charter between Port Townsend and Whidbey Island. Running a ferry operation required the approval of the Territorial legislature – and there was competition for this charter. Captain Elbrecht of Port Townsend almost beat Coupe to the punch. Actually, in the heated competition, Elbrecht did give Coupe an actual punch – or slap on the mouth – which resulted in his arrest, trial, and a fine of $100. Eventually, Captain Elbrecht wearied of the contest and sailed off to the Sandwich Islands as master of the *Toando*.

But Thomas Coupe did not weary on his quest. In 1860, he served as Representative from Island County to the 8th Territorial legislative session. The motivation wasn't necessarily to become a politician. As leaders in a newly-formed county, Coupe and others wisely recognized the necessity of governmental representation. The records show that each eligible man took his turn at office, some liking it more than others. In a January, 1861, letter to Winfield Scott Ebey, Coupe wrote, "I am sick of politics, and I am glad that my time is growing short here. . ." The issue of removal of the Territorial government from Olympia to Vancouver sparked a heated debate that was surely only one of the reasons the Captain longed for the billowing seas rather than the bellow of fellow legislators. One thing had been accomplished: House Bill No. 5, "An act to grant Thomas Coupe the right to establish a ferry between Port Townsend and Whidbey Island."

That same year, 1860, Coupe had an 8.65 ton sloop built and named *Maria* after his daughter. Soon after, he had two other sailing vessels built, *Keturah* and *Mary Ellen*, in honor of two other daughters. The ships worked his Coupe's Express service and his newly-won ferry route.

Sometime after the Civil War, Thomas Coupe commissioned J.F.T. Mitchell of Utsalady to build a steamboat forty-six feet long, with a beam of only ten feet. As originally built, she had no wheelhouse, but was designed to steer with a tiller from a small cabin cockpit. She was, however, well-named the *Success* (after his former ship), for after launching in the spring of 1868, she operated one trip daily between Ebey's Landing, Port Townsend, Port Ludlow and Port Gamble until 1872. On the *Success*, Coupe's son, George, found both his sea legs and his career while serving as deckhand. After the vessel was sold in 1872, she served the Seattle – Port Blakely route under various owners until January 23, 1907, when a storm foundered her while anchored near Madison Park in Seattle.

In 1871 Thomas Coupe took another turn serving on the Washington Territorial Legislature. Even at fifty-three, Coupe probably preferred to be out on his ships. But no doubt the pioneer leaders firmly reminded each other that the work they did would pave the way for future generations on Whidbey Island.

Only four years later, Thomas Coupe died. But remarkable achievements filled his fifty-seven years.

Captain George Marshall Coupe
1849-1937

George Marshall Coupe, born in New York City, May 30, 1849, was the son of Captain Thomas Coupe, and was literally born to the sea. Like his swashbuckling father he was a true pioneer. Like his father, he sailed through the Straits of Magellan from New York to San Francisco, and spent his life on the water as deck hand, engineer, purser and captain.

In 1853, George, his mother, two sister's and a brother boarded the *Thomas Church,* and sailed from New York City, bound for San Francisco to meet his father, with nothing but their bags and a letter of confidence from his sea faring father. On his first trip through the Straits, George, at age four, was not in command and probably was more concerned about his next meal than the reefs on the sails.

The journey around Cape Horn took six months. When they arrived his mother hoisted him over the gunnel to give him his first view of a western boom town, and see his father standing on the deck waiting to greet the family. From here they traveled north to Whidbey Island where Thomas Coupe had found a home, a place to raise his family.

As a lad of eight, he was forever impressed when chilling terror accompanied the raid by the Haidah Indians that resulted in the decapitation of Col. Isaac Ebey, a neighbor. George never forgot the funeral he attended with his father

George's working days on the sea began when he was twelve, serving as a deck hand on his father's sloops, *Maria*, *Keturah* and *Mary Ellen*. All were sailing vessels of moderate size that his father used to haul mail, dry goods, and passengers from Port Townsend to Ebey's Landing on Whidbey Island. But the age of sail was ending and by the time he was nineteen he was working on the steamer *Success*, built for his father at Utsalady.

In those days navigational lights around the sound were few. In 1868 there was a light at Tatoosh, Dungeness, Ediz Hook and Race Rock on Vancouver Island, but no fog horns. Engineer Coupe was working on the tug *Favorite*, when it delieverd the materials for the first fog horn to be installed at Cape Flattery, in 1872. Materials for the installation were brought ashore in canoes, however the boilers floated and were thrust overboard and towed.

He worked his way through the ranks from deck hand to master. He served as engineer on the steamer *Lunnie*, assistant engineer on the *Favorite*, captain of the steamer *Phantom*, and the *James Mattie* in the years between 1872 and 1880.

Later he began working on the Alaska route, serving aboard the steam schooner *Protection*, later on the steamer *Laurada*. When the call of gold was heard in Alaska, George was purser on the steamer *Oregon*, carrying a load of 540 passengers bound for the gold fields.

Captain George Coupe served in every capacity aboard more than a dozen steam ships during a fifty year career that saw Washington move from a Territory to a State.

In 1887 he married Mollie S. Moore and moved to

Seattle. They had four children, Carl, who died at five; Herbert, Rhea and Wallace. Herbert's son Thomas still lives on Whidbey Island.

When Captain George Coupe died, in 1937, a Seattle paper printed Tennyson's *Crossing the Bar,* in tribute, which begins:

Sunset and evening star,

and one clear call for me!

And may there be no moaning of the bar,

When I put out to sea...

Captain Robert C. Fay
Cuttingsville, Vermont
1820 – 1872

Picture courtesy of Island County Historical Society

The adventurous but treacherous life aboard a whaling ship enticed Robert Fay when he was 25 years old. As a mate on the *Harvest*, Fay's first voyage lasted three and one-half years – a short trip by whaling standards, since whalers remained at sea until their holds were full of blubber or sperm oil. Sometimes the men were gone from their families for ten years at a time.

But Robert Fay set out again. The next record finds him in San Francisco ready to sail with Captain Isaiah Folger as master on the schooner *Exact* in 1849. With this ship, Fay shared the distinction of assisting the first settlers to land on Alki Point in 1851, the beginning of Seattle. It may also have been his first exposure to the Native Americans who were to become his friends, and their champion for the remainder of his life.

What is known for certain is that, like so many other sea captains who sailed into Puget Sound in the 1850's, Captain Fay had found home. He remained in the area from that time on. Shipping records in 1855 show Fay was the master of the schooner *A.G. Trask* which docked in Seattle.

Others record Fay's seemingly unique determination to aid anyone in need. He made no distinction between a settler who needed help in building a house or a Native American who needed assistance in understanding and dealing with devastating changes.

These characteristics certainly influenced Fay's appointment as one of the first and most experienced sub-Indian agents in the Washington Territory. His official reports are often in defense of Native Americans who were being taken advantage of by the settlers moving into their territory. In fact, by the 1850's many Native Americans were already living on doles from the government, a welfare system which Fay abhorred. Fay encouraged them to return to making their own living and regain their dignity. Reportedly, he was fairly successful in controlling the sale of liquor which caused so many serious problems.

In 1855-1856 as Indian Agent, Fay is credited with resolving serious conflicts not only between whites and tribes, but also between various tribes, disputing individuals, and government and parties of either side. An Indian agent was on the job 24 hours a day, required to tediously document even the most inconsequential transactions and events, and was the voice of the law.

How did he cope? A jovial disposition probably allowed him to manage an incredibly difficult job. Fay had a reputation for being excellent company. Not only did he have a knack for telling jokes, but also of good naturedly being the butt of pranks. He was the acknowledged champion snorer in the territory, having once spent the night in a home that actually shook with his snoring. When the host went to waken Fay, he found that the snoring had shaken the bed apart. Fay lay in a lump of broken slats and bedding. When awakened, Fay laughed heartily at himself.

In 1860 Fay settled into the life of husband and farmer. After marrying Francis Alexander, the widow of John Alexander who had been one of the first three settlers in the Coupeville area, he moved to his fertile prairie claim near Coveland, on Penn Cove.

Fay continued community service as Superintendent of Common Schools in 1862. He had taken over four school districts, two of which had held no school in the previous year. During his tenure as superintendent, Fay worked to improve the standard of education for all in his school districts.

In 1869 he was appointed County Auditor and Probate Judge, a position he held until his death at age 52. His wife Frances continued to live in Coupeville until her death thirty years later.

Captain Eli Hathaway
(Date of birth and death not known)

Monroe's Landing - Near Hathaway Land Claim

The lives of most pioneer sea captains of Whidbey Island read like adventure stories with happy endings. An exception is the life of Captain Eli Hathaway. He had more than his share of adventures and narrow escapes on Puget Sound, but his luck turned and his last years were most pitiful.

As the master of the schooner *Damaris Cove*, which had docked in Seattle in June 1852, Captain Hathaway rescued gold prospectors when they had been captured by the Haida Indians. On another occasion he rescued Samuel Hancock, a Neah Bay trading post associate, and his crew when their ship was wrecked at Nootka Sound and they were held prisoner by Haidas.

Hathaway had sailed up the coast from San Francisco to Port Townsend with Captain Holbrook. The two subsequently invested in a mainland trading post on south Bellingham Bay. They barely escaped with their lives when a group of Haidas canoed down from northern Vancouver Island and burned the place to the ground.

Moving to Whidbey Island, Captain Hathaway claimed

land behind what is now Monroe's Landing and settled down to farm. But his wife Clarissa, of Cambridge, Massachusetts, never came west to join him there.

From 1864 to 1872, Hathaway was sheriff and assessor for Island County and a respected member of the community. In addition, county records show he was paid for labor in helping to build a jail in 1865 for the island's first murderer.

In 1875 he sold his farm, livestock, and equipment to Dana M. Brown of Thurston County. In 1876 he paid the same Dana Brown $2,000, a lot of money in those days, to provide him for the remainder of his life with food, clothing, and shelter in a manner suitable to his present condition.

In September 1875 Hathaway's farm animals were returned to him. On February 12, 1878, Brown declared the farm a homestead and in April sold it to Ammon Hancock of Lynchberg, Virginia, for $1,800. Hancock never came west and later sold the property to Catherine Monroe. Thus Hathaway's homestead became Monroe's Landing, a dock for a wonderful farm extending to and including the current airport.

In 1880, Hathaway declared himself a pauper and applied to the county commissioners for support. He was one of Island County's first welfare cases. Finally, in 1882, he was declared insane and sent to Steilacoom for his final days.

Many details of Hathaway's life are missing, but here is a sad ending for a respected pioneer sea captain, long time county sheriff, and homesteader who appears to have been swindled by fate – and Mr. Brown.

Captain Richard Blackmer Holbrook
Manomet, Massachusetts
1821 – 1892

Picture courtesy of Island County Historical Society

Following the example of his father, Captain Gideon Holbrook, who served on a ship during the American Revolution when he was 14, Richard Blackmer Holbrook began a life of adventure at sea by joining the fishing fleet off Newfoundland's foggy Grand Banks at the young age of 13.

Later he graduated to whaling ships, making two long voyages of 5 years each. These voyages took him all over the world. On the way to the Pacific Northwest, he rounded Cape Horn and then traveled as far north as the coast of the Kamchatka Peninsula.

On one trip, Holbrook and his crew encountered starvation and disease. When the ship limped into Honolulu, the captain was the only man able to stand at the wheel. His distress signal brought 20 Hawaiian boats to the rescue. While being nursed back to health, captain and crew were entertained by King

Kamehameha IV and Queen Emma.

On another occasion Holbrook voyaged around the Cape of Good Hope in Africa, en route to Canton. In China, he developed an admiration for the people. Years later, when Chinese immigrants living on Whidbey Island were assailed by the locals with vigilante fervor, Holbrook's was a minority voice of reason and justice.

While waiting in New Bedford for a new ship, Captain Holbrook resigned his commission in response to the 1849 Gold Fever and took passage to the San Francisco boom town. He invested his $1,000 savings in a sloop which he sailed up and down the coast from Monterey to San Francisco buying produce and selling it to the hungry masses panning for gold on the Sacramento River. In 1851 he sailed to the Northwest and returned to San Francisco with a load of spars for dock construction.

Ever the adventurer, Holbrook found his way to Port Townsend in 1852 where he met Captain Eli Hathaway. Together they bought a small boat and sailed around Whidbey Island and into Penn's Cove, eventually landing on the northwest bank.

He was so taken by what he saw that he homesteaded 160 acres at San de Fuca and pitched a tent among the wild rose bushes and willows just off the beach. By fall, he had built a small log cabin up the rocky hillside.

Continuing their partnership, Holbrook and Captain Hathaway operated a trading post on Bellingham Bay across from Lummi Island. They stocked everything from gunpowder to a broadcloth dress suit. Each man had invested $1,300 of which each kept $200 in reserve. Hathaway put his money in a safe place in the trading post, but Holbrook kept his in his pocket.

One morning, when they opened for business, they were stunned to see painted braves of the Haida tribe getting out of their canoes. Because Captain Hathaway had twice outwitted the Haidas in their own territory and it appeared the braves wanted revenge, the two captains ran out the back door into the forest, leaving their pipes, coats and hats. Holbrook made his way to safety, clothing torn, hungry and weary, but with his $200 safe in his pocket. A search party found Hathaway with nothing but torn rags on his back. When the men returned to their trading post, they found only smoldering ashes. Hathaway's $200 was gone with the fire.

Not to be deterred, the enterprising Holbrook began logging for spars on Camano Island with a crew of native people. To avoid loss of his land, he proved his claim at San de Fuca and farmed as well. He was later described by his daughter Mollie Frances as an impractical but contented farmer, deeply attached to the land. In fact, every evening in good weather he walked over the hills to enjoy the beautiful view of Penn's Cove and the Cascade and Olympic Mountains. On Christmas Eve, 1860, Holbrook married Harriet Low Sylvester. She had come from Maine by way of the Isthmus of Panama to join her first husband in Olympia. However, she was unable to locate him, and after a few years the legislature annulled the marriage on grounds of desertion.

Holbrook met Harriet Sylvester on a trip to Olympia with Captain Coupe. After a week's courtship, Holbrook and Harriet were married.

They began their marriage by passing through a heavy storm in a canoe on their way to Penn's Cove. Harriet faced the storm without fear and earned the admiration of her husband.

Holbrook could also count on Harriet when it came to farming their 50 acre field: she drove the horses while he held the plow.

At first farming was slow to pay off for the Holbrooks. They garnered more income from selling their mare's yearly colt than from cultivating their fields. But markets – stimulated by a fleet of small steamers to transport goods – were developing from Victoria BC to Tacoma and on to San Francisco. So farming slowly became profitable. And Holbrook continued to master a steamer carrying his wheat or colt to Victoria.

Seven children were born to the Holbrooks on the farm, but only 3 survived to maturity. Son Horace became a carpenter and shipbuilder, and part owner of the Coupeville Mill Company. Another son, Richard, became a sea captain and lived in Seattle. Daughter Mollie Frances, the family historian, graduated from Oberlin College and the Emerson School of Oratory in Boston. She worked as a journalist in New York and Los Angeles and was a published, inspirational poet. She returned to Coupeville in 1937 to care for her ailing brother and remained there until her death in 1953.

Mollie describes her mother Harriet as the kindest of neighbors, and a loyal friend who assisted many babies to be born and many old and young to die with a friendly hand to ease their passage.

Captain Holbrook was active in politics throughout his life, especially behind the scenes lobbying for the interests of Whidbey Island, and the territory. He served at various times as Grand Juror to the U.S. District Court held in Coveland. He also served as treasurer of Island County, and not trusting banks, he kept the county funds in a sugar bowl in the china closet. He served two terms in the Territorial Legislature and was instrumental in opening the mail route between Olympia, Seattle, and Bellingham. He also served as an Assistant Indian Agent under Captain Fay in 1857.

Like most islanders, Holbrook was a staunch Republican. He was a sociable man, had an excellent memory, and was an engaging conversationalist who enjoyed discussing current events, politics, and history.

Late in life the Holbrooks moved to Seattle, where they lost all their possessions in the Great Seattle Fire of 1889. They moved back to Whidbey Island, across the cove from Holbrook's old donation land claim.

In 1892, at the age of 72, Holbrook died. His daughter was most proud of these words in his obituary: "Captain Richard B. Holbrook was a man of absolute integrity."

Harriet followed her husband in death in 1920, at the age of 85.

Captain Simeon Bartlett Kinney
Yarmouth, Nova Scotia
1808 – 1873

Picture courtesy of Island County Historical Society

"Father on his first voyage to Puget Sound was fascinated with the country," wrote daughter Calista. "On his return he said he had found the 'Garden of Eden.'" In his seafaring career he sailed much of the world – voyages from Boston to London, commands on a passenger clipper in the China-East India trade, as well as captaining large vessels out of St. John for many years.

According to Calista, Captain Kinney was a family-loving man, a difficult role for a man who made his living on the sea. In earlier years, his wife Olive accompanied him on foreign voyages whenever she could. The children, as they came along, eagerly awaited Kinney's homecomings, knowing they'd be "lavished with treats." Besides their father's gifts, the children also received "little treasures from around the world" from other sea captains who found the Kinney home a favorite gathering place while in port.

"The days when father's ship was 'in' were the mountain peaks of our childhood days. To father, too, they were days of keen pleasure, for he thoroughly enjoyed his children," Calista remembered. She recalls that she and her sister Marie Antoinette had loved to sing and dance for their father's entertainment.

In 1849, Captain Kinney brought the *Duke of Wellington* from St. John around the Horn on his first trip to San Francisco – a voyage that took eleven months. Knowing this would be a long and lonely trip, but unable to accompany her husband, Olive smuggled daughter Frances aboard to keep her father company. It was a voyage fraught with potential frights and dangers, nevertheless an exciting adventure for a child.

Sadly, before Captain Kinney could return home from that journey, he received word that his wife had died. Two of Kinney's six surviving children were old enough to be on their own, so he made arrangements and paid $250 apiece for Olive Jane (Jennie) to bring the three youngest children, ranging in age from 10 to 14, to San Francisco to join him and their sister Frances. Jennie must have struggled mightily to comply with her father's wishes. She was only 21 years old, married to a husband who was away at sea, had a two-year-old daughter of her own, and was six months pregnant.

Bravely, Jennie, with her daughter Susie, sisters Calista and Marie Antoinette, and brother Bob embarked on the *George Raynes*, a three-masted, full-rigged ship, for the trip to San Francisco. The voyage took more than four months. Calista wrote in her journal, "Because of scarcity of water, no washing of clothes could be done, so it had been necessary to plan for a large supply, enough to permit a change every two weeks."

One can only imagine the joy and relief of the reunited family, plus one, Georgia McKinnon, named for the ship on which she was born. "Immediately we made our home on father's ship, the *Rosalind*, lying at anchor in the harbor," Calista wrote. "He tried to see that his daughters were trim, neat and ladylike." Before going out on a pleasure trip, he would have a formal inspection of his daughters and say, "Let us see if you are all square by your lifts and braces."

Three months later, the Captain sold the *Rosalind* and moved the family to a little cottage on Second Street in San Francisco. There were no sidewalks, the surrounding hills

110

were covered with lupine, and in the harbor, many ships lay idle and rotting. They were deserted by their captains and crew who had taken off for the gold mines. Later, Captain Kinney moved his family to one of those ships, the *Plieades*, an old whaler from New Bedford.

Marie's turn to adventure with her father – on a commercial voyage around the world – came next. She wrote about the thrill of being entertained by handsome sailors on many British and American warships, and of meeting in China the preacher brother of Harriet Beecher Stowe. He was holding services in a houseboat where Marie willingly sang and took part.

After Kinney decided he'd had his fill of long voyages to foreign ports, he sailed between San Francisco and Puget Sound. In the spring of 1854, Calista accompanied her father on one of the trips aboard his ship, the *Burnham*, loaded with merchandise for a little store on Penn's Cove. The voyage took about two weeks. Of this trip, Calista wrote, "Our ships 'entering' was recorded at Port Townsend, and then we sailed to Penn's Cove, a trading post on Whidbey Island, where we unloaded part of our cargo. There were great stretches of quiet water, shores densely wooded, with firs dipping down to the tide-regulated beaches, and along the shores, Indian camps, often evidenced only by the canoes drawn up out of the reach of the tide. Here we visited at the cabin of Captain Coupe. . . . There was a large settlement of Indians near, and I'll admit I was afraid though the Sound Indians had the reputation of being peace-loving."

After delivering supplies to Coupeville, Captain Kinney and Calista continued on to Utsalady on Camano Island. While the Burhham was loading pilings, Calista made friends with the Indians who came aboard and gathered around her. They were so eagerly curious to touch and examine everything about her that she finally realized (and later confirmed) she was the first white woman to reach the shores of Camano Island.

During the last stage of Captain Kinney's seafaring career, he went back to San Francisco and served as Harbor Master of San Francisco Bay, a post he held until his death. He left six sons and daughters, twenty grandchildren, and a number of great grandchildren.

In his obituary, a San Francisco newspaper reported, "Captain Simeon B. Kinney, one of the early pioneers of California, died at his residence on Post Street, San Francisco, on Sunday morning, June 7, 1873, in the sixty-seventh year of his age. Capt. Kinney was widely and favorably known as one of the oldest and ablest shipmasters of this coast."

Captain Thomas Franklin Kinney
St. John, New Brunswick
1829 – 1903

Picture courtesy of Island County Historical Society

Thomas Kinney, the son of a sea captain, first sailed with his father at the age of seven. Leaving his childhood home, he went to sea at 16, became a mate on a West India brig at 18, and first mate of a whaling ship at 19. At 21, he became a sea captain in his own right. While little is reflected in family history of Kinney's early years, clearly, he took every opportunity to be on or near the water in his adult life.

Thomas Kinney was born the first of eight children of Simeon Bartlett Kinney and Olive Doane Kinney. Even though he sailed from his home for ports such as Liverpool and San Francisco, he continued to return to the area of his birth and on March 20, 1858, married Mary Elizabeth Houghton, a native of Nova Scotia. October 14, 1859, their only child, Julia, was born at Mary's parents' home at Hall's Harbour, Cornwallis, Nova Scotia.

When Julia was four, the family moved to Yarmouth, Nova Scotia. According to a letter written by his sister Mizie Hackett (Marine Antoinette Kinney) to their father Simeon Kinney, January 8, 1865, Thomas had been running a small vessel carrying potatoes to and around St. John:

"As usual, he has had "bad luck" as he calls it, and been frozen up in the snow, where his eyes became very sore, and he had to walk from "Corn Wallis" to Yarmouth, a hundred and fifty miles in the dead of winter. He found his little girl just recovering from typhoid and his wife was taken, immediately after with the same disease, though she was better when he wrote."

At some point in this time period, Kinney made the decision to move his family to the more mild climate of Penn's Cove on Whidbey Island.

Kinney had first come to Whidbey in 1852. From 1852 to 1854, he had been mate on the *Chalcedony*, a bark captained by his brother-in-law Howard Bentley Lovejoy, and made several trips to Snakelum Point where he loaded spars bound for San Francisco. While the 5'8" Kinney was loading these spars, his physical strength was observed by the local members of the Snohomish tribe, and they nicknamed him "Skoodnum," meaning strong.

In 1868, when Kinney was working at the Mare Island Navy Yard, Mary and Julia left New York for San Francisco via the Isthmus of Panama. They crossed the isthmus on a narrow-gauge train. En route, Elizabeth bought Julia a parrot and a parakeet. Julia would later remember that this parrot "would perch on father's shoulder at breakfast and drink coffee."

After his wife and daughter (with parrot and parakeet) arrived in San Francisco, they went to live for two years with Kinney's father in Potrero, a suburb of that city. Meanwhile, Kinney had bought property and built a home for his family on the corner of what is currently Front and Kinney streets in Coupeville.

In May 1871, after being sent for and traveling for nearly a month on Simeon's bark *Onward*, Mary and Julia arrived at Utsalady on Camano Island. Kinney met his family at Utsalady, loaded their household goods and other belongings onto a big dory, and rowed all to their new home on Penn's Cove.

Once his family was settled in Coupeville, Kinney mastered the trading schooner *Shoo Fly* on Puget Sound for eight years. After selling the schooner in 1882, he finally retired from the sea. But on land, he built four more houses near his own, all of which are still standing.

Even though he retired from the sea, Kinney's habits as a sailing shipman were legendary – at least among the young boys in town. Remembering his great uncle, Mike Lovejoy writes:

"He wore gold earrings and had a complete vocabulary of all the cuss words that ever existed. On the beach below his home on Front Street, he built a bulkhead of logs as underpinning for a platform to build boats. He was a powerful man and lifted those logs – one end at a time. We kids in the town when we went by on the bank above always threw rocks down on him just to hear him cuss, and the madder he got the more he cussed."

However, family historians are quick to add that Kinney never used this language around his wife and daughter.

After more than 30 years of stable and somewhat colorful living on Whidbey Island, what Kinney had referred to as his bad luck returned. Mary died on July 7, 1900, having been sick for the greater part of three years. Then, Kinney contracted lip cancer caused by the pipe tobacco he continually smoked, and he died in Coupeville on March 21, 1903.

Captain Howard Bentley Lovejoy
Kennebec County, Maine
1827 – 1872

Picture courtesy of Island County Historical Society

Howard Bentley Lovejoy's farflung seafaring spanned Mexico, Bolivia, Russia, and Alaska. He encountered war, bounty, and shipwreck. As a young man of 19, who had been raised in Milltown, New Brunswick, he enlisted in the U.S. Navy. He immediately became a gunner in the Mexican War during the capture of Veracruz. But war did not appeal to young Lovejoy, so he took his share of the bounty and headed back home to Milltown.

In 1849 news of the California Gold Rush swept the land, enticing many young men to "go west." Still looking for adventure, Lovejoy caught the gold fever and struck out from Maine, with a party of 22 other young men, to seek his fortune. But he spent only a short time mining before the sea called him out of San Francisco aboard a ship bound for southern ports.

Lovejoy came to Whidbey Island as captain of the *Chalce-*

dony with Thomas Kinney as his mate. In Penn's Cove, they loaded the bark with spars for docks to be built in San Francisco. On later voyages, they loaded spars from Long Point and Snakelum Point.

On one of his voyages to Penn's Cove, Lovejoy was introduced to Captain Simeon Bartlett Kinney's daughter, Calista, who had sailed to Whidbey Island with her father from their home in San Francisco. It was raining when they met, and Calista feared damage to her black silk dress and yellow silk bonnet. With his mackintosh, Captain Lovejoy came gallantly to her rescue. Later, Calista recalled how often she laughed at the figure she must have cut at their first meeting.

After that, Captain Lovejoy often visited Calista when in port. Calista didn't take his attentions seriously. She was only seventeen, and Captain Lovejoy was ten years her senior. But she enjoyed his company, and he was very handsome and a striking six feet tall. On one outing, Lovejoy took a party, which included Calista, over to Sausalito to view a brig and an Admiral's ship that had come in from the Crimean War. There, his attentions finally paid off. When Captain Lovejoy again sailed away, he was engaged to Calista.

On January 8, 1855, Calista and Lovejoy set sail from San Francisco on their honeymoon. His ship, the *Chalcedony*, was bound for the Russian village of Sitka, Alaska – twelve years before the United States purchased Alaska from the Russians. She was loaded with a cargo of wheat, hides, and tallow. The wheat was to be ground in mills at Sitka and the *Chalcedony* was to return to San Francisco with some of the flour, along with furs, ice, and salmon.

There were no lighthouses or other navigational aids to guide them on their voyage to Sitka. Existing charts were imperfect. After a very rough trip, they reached the entrance of Sitka Harbor, only to be mistaken for a man-of-war. No pilot would venture out to guide a warship in, yet the wind was blowing so fiercely it was impossible to anchor where they were. As the intensity of the wind increased, they were forced to put back out to sea, dangerously buffeted by the terrifying gales so common in the North Pacific winters. It was two weeks before they sighted Sitka again. This time, after they fired their cannon, the famous Russian tug, *Politkofsky*, responded. With the tug's help, the *Chalcedony* finally made her way safely into the harbor at Sitka.

Sitka was just a tiny Russian village at that time, and apparently Calista was the first American woman to visit Alaskan shores. Looking back at herself as a bride of seventeen, she said of the voyage, "I often wonder that I felt no fear in undertaking a voyage to far away Alaska, an almost uncharted coast, an almost unknown country and in the dead of winter. But I loved the sea and I had implicit confidence in my husband."

Calista and the first of her seven children lived on the "shores densely wooded" of Whidbey Island for a short time in the late 1850's. A letter to Calista, dated September 1858, shows Captain Lovejoy was in British Columbia, wanting to try his luck in the Fraser River Gold Rush. But around 1860 Captain Lovejoy was back in the shipping business running a schooner from Mazatlan to La Paz and back loaded with cargoes of shells.

During this time, Calista moved the family back to San Francisco. Lovejoy sorely missed seeing his family. There was no opportunity to get to San Francisco between voyages. When he became sick, he took action, completed a final run, gathered the family, and returned to Whidbey Island.

He settled them on a 134 acre homestead at Lovejoy's Point, adjoining Captain Coupe's homestead on the east. President U.S. Grant signed deeds for the homestead and donation claims, deeds still in the possession of his great granddaughter. At that time, the properties of Coupe, Lovejoy, and Alexander comprised the total site of Coupeville.

His family in place, Captain Lovejoy began making long voyages for the Hudson Bay Company. This left Calista alone with the children. Though having a good relationship with the local Native Americans, Calista feared raids from the fierce

Haidas – and even some of the local men when they were drunk. Aware of her fear, the eighteen year old son of Chief Squi Squi appointed himself protector of Calista, sleeping across the entrance of her cabin doorway.

Wanting to be closer to his family and perhaps because of Calista's uneasiness, Lovejoy took a job as one of the first pilots in Puget Sound. He did an early-day "commute" to Utsalady or Ebey's Landing then on to Port Townsend where he boarded incoming ships to guide them into their ports.

An 1868 letter to Captain Simeon B. Kinney in San Francisco states that Captain Lovejoy was running the steam ferry *Success* for Captain Coupe from Port Townsend to the island. Of this venture he commented, "I am kept so busy I have no time for anything. It keeps me from town in the morning till eight at night to get through my work. I have everything to do, captain, purser, engineer, fireman [wood-burning steamer]. So, I'm kept busy. The boat does not steam fast! It takes me 3 hours from Ludlow to Port Townsend, 2-1/2 hours from Port Townsend to Landing [Ebey's] and back to Port Townsend, back to Ludlow the same day."

In addition to being a deeply religious man, Lovejoy was also a member of the Good Templars Lodge. Perhaps the strain of such heavy responsibilities contributed to Captain Lovejoy's death at only forty-five. He left his young wife and six surviving children in their isolated pioneer home, watched over by fatherly neighbor Captain Coupe.

One son, Howard Lovejoy, built many of the fine homes in Coupeville, the original Coupeville courthouse, and several boats, including the *Calista*. In later years, he assisted his own son in starting the Puget Sound Freight Lines in Seattle.

Two more generations carried on the seafaring tradition. Calista and Howard Bentley Lovejoy's son, Captain Laurin Bentley Lovejoy, and their grandsons, Captain Bartlett Lovejoy, and Captain Stanley T. Lovejoy, all became ship pilots in Puget Sound.

Captain George Morse
Brunswick Maine
1830 – 1915

Picture courtesy of Island County Historical Society

At 28 years, Captain Morse, just a "youngster," settled in Oak Harbor, but not until he'd experienced a lifetime of adventures around the world. By then, he had worked alongside his father in the shipbuilding trade for eight years, so his skills were sufficiently honed to sail as ship's carpenter around the Horn to San Francisco and on to Australia and England.

Impressed by prospects of the Gold Rush, he headed back to California by way of Nicaragua. In California, he was not only lucky in mining gold, but was also serious-minded enough not to gamble it all away, saving instead to buy a pack train of substantial size. With this, he forsook the caprices of the Gold Rush for a more certain income provisioning the California mining camps with supplies they so desperately lacked. After seven years, his already well-developed business sense led him on to fresher needs at the newly discovered Fraser River mines. Then while wintering-over by the Nooksack River in the Washington Territories, he sold his pack train and joined a crew surveying the forty-ninth parallel.

Resurrecting his old trade, he settled in Whatcom (Bellingham) long enough to help build the schooner *General Harney*. From there he was hired to help build the schooner *Growler* for Captain Barrington in Oak Harbor.

He had finally discovered Whidbey Island. He liked the fertile land and determined to eventually settle there, but he first took appointments as sub-Indian agent at La Conner and then Tulalip. While at Tulalip, he constructed buildings for Father Chirouse's school and married a Native American woman by whom he had a daughter, Nellie.

But ships lured him onward, so he left his family, bought the schooner *Granger*, and sailed between Puget Sound and British Columbian ports, with an occasional foray to Alaska. Between wanderings, he returned to Whidbey Island to a farm near Oak Harbor that was to become his permanent home.

In 1866 he married Mary O'Leary whose first husband had been drowned off Blower's Bluff. He became father to her children, and they added five more of their own.

Needing to accommodate his growing family, he made use of his carpenter skills and built what later became known as the "Morse Mansion." With a huge kitchen, pantry, dining room with a fireplace, curved stairways, four bedrooms, and inlaid parquet floors, it indeed qualified as a "mansion" in those days.

As Captain Morse retired from the sea, he threw the weight of all his previous skills and business acumen into the community of Oak Harbor. In addition to raising fine horses, he owned a store, a wharf, a hotel, and a blacksmith shop there. In recognition of his outstanding dedication to the community, he was elected county commissioner. That proved to be only the beginning of his political career. When Washington became a state, Morse was elected to the first state legislature and then was reelected for three more terms.

While he was serving in the legislature, he lobbied to implement his most farsighted dream – a bill for $20,000 to build approaches to a bridge across Deception Pass. The bill passed but the young state had no money to back it up. The best that could be done was to build a miniature of the proposed span and display it at the Alaska-Yukon Exposition in 1909. Who but a man of great vision could have foreseen the need for a bridge to a wilderness island with a scattering of tiny settlements? Local author Dorothy Neil notes that Morse's daughter, Sadie Morse Davis, vividly remembered many times as a child sailing through Deception Pass with her father as he told how tiny Pass Island would make the perfect pier for a bridge which would someday be built to Whidbey Island.

In 1915, twenty years before the bridge was completed, Captain Morse died. But during the construction of the bridge, his grave in the Oak Harbor Pioneer Cemetery was scattered with rock taken from the Whidbey side of Deception Pass in remembrance of his vision for Island County.

Captain James H. Swift
Middleboro, Massachusetts
1816 – 1892

Picture courtesy of Island County Historical Society

Could his birth on the Fourth of July have been the spark igniting a life of adventure? Fireworks would seem a fitting welcome for a lad who ran off to sea at fourteen, rose quickly from cabin boy to mate and made master by the age of twenty-one. James Swift sailed the world seven times and spent eight years in Arctic waters. He married three times and had ten children and was active in politics and social events. And when he finally left the sea, he had an enjoyable run as "gentleman farmer."

During Swift's years in the Arctic, he brought back to his New Bedford port one record-breaking load of 3,500 barrels of oil. He set another record after he began to sail the waters of Puget Sound: U.S. Custom records of 1855 credit Swift with delivering the first foreign consignment from this area to a European port – a cargo of spars from Camano Island shipped aboard Swift's bark *Anadir* to naval shipyards in Brest, France. On a subsequent trip to Europe, Swift sold the *Anadir* after delivering her load of spars to the British Navy in Falmouth. As master of the *Anadir, George, Nebraska,* and the clipper *Formosa,* Swift sailed into all the major ports of the world.

During his Northwest travels Swift became enamored with the beauty of the Puget Sound area, particularly Whidbey Island. In 1858 his enthusiasm for the "most beautiful place he had ever seen" prompted him to buy the Jacob Smith Donation Claim on the north shore of Penn's Cove for $3,000 in gold sovereigns. However, the ill health of his first wife had prevented her and their three children from traveling west, so Swift didn't actually take up his claim until after his wife's death.

In 1863 Swift and his new 18-year-old bride, Louise Butler, sailed for Whidbey Island on their wedding trip. Swift's son, who was only two years younger than his stepmother, accompanied them. Daughter Hattie finished school in the East and, along with Louise's younger sister, Annie Butler, joined them later.

When Captain Swift and Louise arrived at Utsalady in 1863, they had the advantage of bringing on the ship many of the comforts of home. Theirs would be a life of relative ease among the settlers.

While her stepson thought it "Godforsaken country," Louise's letters home reveal an enthusiasm for Whidbey Island that matched her husband's, perhaps because they led such an active social life. In 1864, she wrote of a schooner launched from the island to which they were invited for cake and wine, commenting, "It was a nice time. We have more balls in this country than at home and always have a supper."

Louise gave birth to two sons, Charles and Edward, who played with the Native American children on the farm where Captain Swift raised horses for the Hudson Bay Company of Victoria. In fact, the chief of the Skagit tribe lived with and worked for the Swifts.

After Hattie arrived from the East, she, too, was enchanted with the island, writing "This is the most elegant and romantic scenery. . . the mountains are glorious and the forests elegant." She married Sam D. Howe, a member of the territorial legislature, and looked forward to an active social season in Olympia. But, tragically, before she and Howe were able to move to Olympia, both she and her step-mother, Louise, died in the diphtheria epidemic of 1869.

In 1870, as Captain of the bark *Aid*, Swift took to the sea again, sailing for the Sandwich Islands. That same year he married for the third time. He and Emily Wilson had five children and named their first child Hattie for her half-sister, a common practice in those days when death struck frequently and early. Hattie was often allowed to accompany her father on shorter trips. He visited old friends, and she was privy to many exciting tales of whaling days, escapes from cannibals, and stories of glamorous ports around the world.

In retirement, ships' captains had a somewhat easier life than their neighbors who depended on farms for their livelihood. James and Emily were no different. They often traveled by canoe, sometimes as far as Victoria, to attend balls, fancy clothes were wrapped in oilskins to protect them from salt water, while Native Americans manned the oars and skillfully navigated the often treacherous waters.

Of Captain Swift's children, one, Arthur, wrote pioneer sketches using the name *Ancutty Tillicum*. Another followed in his father's seafaring footsteps to become Captain Edward Swift, and George, another, became a surgeon in Seattle.

As for Captain James Swift, he continued his active life as a member of the legislature and served on the first Pilot Commission for the Territory from 1878 to 1886, when it disbanded. In his later years he was partially paralyzed, but since he had never yet sat idly around, he had himself wheeled about Coupeville in a wheelbarrow.

Captain William J. Robertson
Norfolk, Virginia
1809 – 1888

Picture courtesy of Island County Historical Society

William Robertson inherited the legacy of a fighting spirit from the Scottish Clan Robertsons, who emigrated from Scotland when clans were outlawed after the bloody Battle of Culloden. His father, a medical doctor, settled the family in Virginia where William was born. Little is known of Robertson's youth; although, family histories include the rumor that young William John ran away to sea and became a Captain at nineteen.

At age twenty-four, Robertson joined his family's fiery spirit with that of the Pierre's, French Huguenots who had escaped to Londonderry fleeing French persecution. The family changed its name when they immigrated to Norfolk where Robertson met and married sixteen-year-old Mary Jane Perry.

After the couple moved to Baltimore, Robertson became involved in shipping and transportation along the Atlantic coast. He is credited with organizing the first Odd Fellows Lodge there – and another when they moved to San Francisco.

Shortly after gold was discovered in California, Robertson chartered a vessel and sailed around Cape Horn to San Francisco – but not because he was afflicted with gold fever like so many ships' officers and crews who left their ships rotting in the harbor. Instead, his vision was of unparalleled business opportunities. Not a single wharf had yet been built in San Francisco Bay to receive cargo for the incessant demands of the mines and miners. Robertson first met the immediate need by procuring two vessels to shuttle the cargo between ships and the shore. Then in 1851 he tackled the long-term demand for pilings for wharves. He purchased the brig *Tarquina* and sailed off to Puget Sound, where he loaded a cargo of pilings from Cape Flattery and returned to San Francisco.

Since he could now anticipate steady work there, Captain Robertson sent for Mary Jane and their five children, ages nine to fourteen. They bravely traveled to San Francisco from New York via the Isthmus of Panama, a treacherous jungle crossing in the days of yellow fever and before the transisthmus railroad was completed in 1855. Reaching the Pacific side, they waited a week for the steamer *Constitution*. After a brief stop in Acapulco, they docked in San Diego for water. Mrs. Robertson attended a dinner in San Diego's "Old Town" before they continued on. Despite the long trip and the dangers, the family was waiting for Captain Robertson in San Francisco when he returned from his second run to Puget Sound for pilings.

Robertson apparently liked what he saw as he sailed along the west side of Whidbey Island. Above Admiralty Inlet spread prairie land for farming and thick forests to supply timber for the piers and mines. Under the Oregon Land Act of 1850, he filed a Land Donation Claim for property at that spot then brought his son John north to secure and work the property. Robertson himself continued the life of a sea captain on the *Tarquina* for another year. Two years later the rest of the family was finally moved to Whidbey Island.

About this time a general unrest brewed among local Native Americans. Just in case he needed it to protect his family and home, Captain Robertson had the small cannon unloaded from his ship and brought to his property. Staying behind to make sure his family was secure, he sent the *Tarquina*, loaded with cargo, to the Sandwich Islands in the charge of his first officer. Robertson never saw the ship again. The mate, taking advantage of his situation, sold the ship, pocketed the $30,000, and disappeared.

With that experience, Captain Robertson decided to put his seafaring days behind him. He worked full time on his property, "Lea Bluffs," until 1859 when he was appointed the first keeper of the new lighthouse. The locals called it "Kellogg Point," but since the lighthouse was only three miles away from Robertson's home, he always referred to it as the "Lea Bluffs Lighthouse." Today it is known as the Fort Casey Lighthouse. Robertson served there five years until Daniel Pearson was appointed keeper by the new Lincoln administration.

Meanwhile, a situation had developed that would span ten years, bringing out both the best and the worst in Robertson – his generosity and his fiery fighting spirit. Captain Robertson had met Charles Sebert and his wife Caroline in San Francisco. As they were interested in a donation claim, Robertson had brought the couple to Whidbey Island on the *Tarquina*. Robertson instructed Sebert on claim procedures and pointed out some good locations for a claim. Allowing the Seberts to stay with his son John and the two men who were employed to work the property, Robertson delivered his goods to the area and picked up cargo for his next trip south.

Before heading out to San Francisco, Captain Robertson inquired if Sebert had selected a claim site, and Sebert replied that he didn't have the money to take up a claim. So Robertson dismissed one of the men working on his property and hired Sebert. Next Sebert wondered where he and his wife would stay. As the Robertson's log cabin had been burned by the natives, John and the hired men had been living in a shanty that was too small for anyone else. But Robertson generously suggested the Sebert use some of his lumber to put up another shanty.

While the trusting Captain Robertson sailed away to San Francisco, young John Robertson was told that his father had instructed Sebert to build a house 200 yards from Robertson's shanty. This he proceeded to do. When Captain Robertson returned from his voyage, he was understandably infuriated at the obvious encroachment on his property. As Robertson thundered that they would have to move, Sebert replied that his wife was pregnant. Robertson relented, noting, "I remarked my object was to assist my fellow man not to distress him and gave him permission to remain there until his wife got well. He said that he would then move from my place. But on my next voyage told me he would not move from there as he had as good a right to it as me."

According to Kellogg's *A History of Whidbey Island,* Robertson now took action in keeping with his fighting ancestry. The captain picked up the *Tarquina's* small brass cannon sitting by his doorway, carried it to the Sebert house, loaded the cannon, and demanded that the house be vacated or he would blow it up. Sebert was away at the time, but Mrs. Sebert stood in the doorway with her baby and challenged Robertson to carry out his threats. Robertson backed down.

However, for Robertson to give up this property would be to lose roughly one-third of his holdings, including prime grazing land and water access to his property: ". . .That portion where Sebert would wish to drive me to the tide flows against the bank making it impassable at high waters for anything that does not wish to swim," as Captain Robertson wrote to Congressman William Wallace, arguing his defense. But whether from tardy guilt or fear that the captain might change his mind about using the cannon, by the time the letter reached its destination, Sebert was building a new house just beyond the claim – then sold it before long to Powell Johnson. Sebert also sold 160 acres of his property to young John Robertson who deeded it to his mother.

Sometime later Robertson returned to the sea and became one of the first Puget Sound pilots. Captain Robertson probably sailed his own sloop over to meet sailing ships at Port Townsend, the only port of entry in Puget Sound. There he boarded incoming ships, took over as captain and navigated through the treacherous tides and currents of the sound.

Captain Robertson continued to oversee his property until his death at seventy-nine in son John Robertson's home in Coupeville.

At one time, John owned most of Coupeville, building a store, wharf, warehouse, and other buildings on front Street and providing the financing for the Glenwood Hotel.

Chapter Eight

THE PRESENT AND THE FUTURE

Today the ships still come, the motor sailors, the power boats, the tugs, and the commercial fishing boats. Boats and ships of every size from small skiffs with outboards, to huge container vessels carrying the goods of trade. Many still carry the products of commerce, but most come with amateur sailors out to participate in a regatta at Oak Harbor, to explore our beaches and inlets, and to try their luck at angling for less abundant fish.

Commercial traffic passes by Whidbey Island through the Strait of Juan de Fuca enroute to Canada, Alaska and the orient; and between Whidbey and Camano in search of recreation. Many a working dock is now a place for pleasure boats to tie up for the night, with shops and services near by.

Whidbey Islands isolation was broached when one of the dreams of early Sea Captains was realized with the building of the Deception Pass Bridge in the 1930's connecting the island to Fidalgo Island and the mainland. To the south bigger and faster ferries carry an ever increasing load of tourists and residents.

Grand dreams of great cities and railroads never came about, for which modern residents are grateful. Caring people have worked to preserve the fertile, rare prairie in central Whidbey. Many of the homes of our early sea captains still stand in their town, Coupeville. A feeling of the past is here and scenes of early history all around from Col. Ebey's home above Ebey's landing, to the blockhouses built to protect against the natives. Fort Casey's old battlements speak of a time when the only threat to the security of the straits came by water.

In the coming years the growth of population is the greatest threat. Talk of a ferry between Camano and Whidbey is often revived.

Whidbey Island was once considered the second largest Island in the contiguous United States, but is now considered the largest since Long Island in New York State was declared a peninsula. Fifty miles long, our island provides many contrasts, and challeneges

The rich heritage of the pioneers is all around in the names of streets and towns: Power, Zylstra, and Engle Roads; Race Lagoon, Lake Hancock and Kennedy Lagoon to name a few. Many decendents of early settlers still live in all areas, from north to south. For the people of today, this look back into the past can help us understand and plan for the future. A future just as full of challenge as that of the early settlers and just as important.

SAILS, STEAMSHIPS & SEA CAPTAINS
BIBLIOGRAPHY

Sea Captain of Whidbey Island - Cahail, Alice Kellogg, 1984, 2nd printing, Daughters of the Pioneers of Washington

A Particular Friend, Penn's Cove, A History of the Settlers, Claims and Buildings of Central Whidbey Island, Cook, Jimmie Jean, 1973, Island County Historical Society, Coupeville

A History of Whidbey Island, Kellogg, George Albert, 1934, Island County Historical Society, Coupeville

Disaster Log of Ships, Gibbs, Jim, 1971, Superior Press Company, Seattle

By Canoe and Sailing Ship They Came, A history of Whidbey's Island, 1989, spindrift Publishing Company, Oak Harbor

Wooden Ship, the building of a wooden sailing vessel 1870 - Jan Adkins, 1978

History of Washington, Idaho, & Montana 1845-1889, Bancroft, San Francisco: The History Company, 1890

Uttermost Part of the Earth, Bridges, Lucas E., New York: E P Dutton Co., 1949

Gold is the Corner Stone, Caughey, John W., Berkly & Los Angeles: University of Cal. press, 1948, 57

Greyhounds of the Sea, Cutler, Carl C. 1960

Two Years Before the Mast, Dana, Richard Henry, Jr. 1836

The Fourth Corner - Highlight from the Early Northwest, Edsoon, Lelah Jackson, Bellingham Wa.: Cox Brothers, Inc.

Further Reading, Journal of the West, Bauer, K.J. and Gilbert, B. F.., Jly 1981

Marine History of the Pacific Northwest, Lewis & Dryden,

Seattle, Superior Publishing Co., 1967

Marine History of the Pacific Northwest, McCurdy, H. W.., Seattle: Superior Publishing Co.

History of the State of Washington, Meany, Edmond S., New York: The MacMillan Co., 1950

Living Pioneers of Washington, Meany, Edmund S, Seattle PI,July 4, 1919

By Sea to San Francisco 1849-59: The Journal of Dr. James Morison, Morison, James, Edit. Connie J. White & William R. Gillaspie, Memp[his State University Press, 1977

National Archives - Seattle Branch, Record Group No. 36, Series 20, Vol 1, October 1853 - June 1861. Series 17,Vol. 2 *Register o fEntrances and Clearances of Vessels,,* 1851-1913

National Archives - The Collection of Customs, Puget Sound District - R.G. 36, Series 26, Vol. 7, 1858-1866

Master Whidbey Proved the Deception, Perkins, Lois Jean, Sea & Pacific Motor Boat, pp 36, Sept. 1965

Pioneer Days on Puget Sound, Seattle: Alice Harrison & Co., 1908

Puget Sound Weekly Courier, Obituary: January 1876, col.1, pp3

San Francisco Ship Passenger Lists, Rasmussen, Louis J., Colman, Cal: San Francisco Historic Records, 1965

Famous Pioneer Steamboats of Puget Sound - Thorniley, William O., July 25, 1925, pp 2-3

Diary of Winfield Scott Ebey, University of Washington of Washington, December 1858-1860, U of W Library, MSSS papers from the Ebey Collection

The Steamer Success, Washington Standard, February 13, 1869, col 5, pp 2

Captain Thomas Coupe: Whidbey Island Pioneer and Captain George Coupe: Continuing the Pioneer Tradition - George D. Obermiller

Washington, Images of a State's Heritage, Carlos Schwantes, Katherine Morrissey, David Nicandri, Susan Strasser, 1988, Melior Publications, Spokane

The Pacific Northwest, an Over-All Appreciation, Edited by Otis W. Freeman and Howard H. Martin, 2nd edition, 1954, John Wiley & Sons, Inc., New York

When Clipper ships Ruled the Seas. James McCague, 1968, Gerrard Publishing Co., Champaign, Illinois

Maritime Memories of Puget Sound, Jim Gibbs and Joe Williamson, 1987, Schiffer Publishing Ltd, West Chester, Pa.

Where Mountains Meet the Sea, An Illustrated History of Puget Sound, James R. Warren, 1986, Windsor Publications, Inc., Northridge, Ca.

Otter Skins, Boston ships, and China Goods: The Martime Trade of the Northwest Coast, 1785-1841, James R. Gibson, 1992, McGill Queen's University Press

Steamers Wake, Jim Faber, 1985, Enetai Press, Seattle

The History of American Sailing Ships, Howard I. Chapelle, 1935, W.N. Norton,NY

Pacific Square Riggers, Jim Gibbs, 1977, Bonanza Books, NY

Trade War: Greed, Power and Industrial Policy on Opposite Sides of the Pacific, Steven Schlostein (sic, 3s's), 1984, Martin Press, NY

The Pacific Rim Almanac, ed Alexander Becher, *The Pacific Ocean,* Gary A. Klee, 1991, Harper Collins, NY

West Coast Windjammers, Jim Gibbs, 1968, Superior Publishing Co., Seattle

Pathfinders in the North Pacific, Marius Barbeau, 1958, Caxton Printer, Ltd., Caldwell, Idaho

The Unusual Side of the Sea, A Slop Chest of Sea Lore, Jim Gibbs, 1971, Windward Publishing Company, Seattle

The History of American Sailing Ships, Howard I. Chapelle, 1935, W.W. Norton and Co., Inc., NY

American Ships, Alexander Laing, 1971, American Heritage Press, NY

Washington, A Bicentennial Hitory, Norman H, Clark, 1976, W.W. Norton & Co., NY

Heritage of the West, Charles Phillips, 1992, Random House, NY

Puget Sound, A Narrative of Early Tacoma and the Southern Sound, Murray Morgan, 1979, University of Washington Press, Seattle

Experience in a Promised Land, edited by G. Thomas Edwards and Carlos A. Schwantes, 1986, University of Washinton Press

Mill Town, Norman H. Clark, 1970, University of Washington Press, Seattle

Handbook of Northwest Indian - Smithsonian.

Swans Among the Indians, Lucille McDonald

Sea Captains of Whidbey Island, Alice Kellogg Cahail, published by the daughters of Pioneers of Washington

Tails from a Seafaring Family, Pioneer Stories, Lillian Dean Huffstetler, The State Association of the Daughters of the Pioneers of Washington, 1986

Excerpts from personal diaries and letters:

Letters to Jane Jones and Karen Erbland, Lillian Dean Huffstetler, January 18, 1993

Personal Journal, Calista Kinney Lovejoy

Letter to Leah Jean Lovejoy, Mike Lovejoy, July 3, 1974

Letter to Leah Jean Lovejoy, Mike Lovejoy, October 16, 1974

Letter to Simeon B. Kinney Marie Antoinette Kinney, January 8, 1865

Robertson Story, Leah Jean Lovejoy

Biography of Captain J. Barrington, Peggy Darst Townsdin

Family History and Letters as saved and passed down, by Christina McCrohan Barrington, Sibella Barrington Fisher and Madeline Fisher Darst

Pfeiffer, Frances Holbrook, monographs on each of her parents written about 1952 commemorating the centennial of his coming to Whidbey Island and her 1855 arrival in the new Washington Territory

U nder the wide and starry sky,
Dig the grave and let me die,
Glad did I live and gladly die.
And I laid me down with a will,

This is the verse you grave for me:
Here he lies where he longed to be;
Home is the sailor, home from the sea,
And the hunter home from the hill.

Requiem, Robert Louis Stevenson

Have you been at sea
* on a windy day*
When the water's blue
And the sky is too,
And showers of spray
Come sweeping the
* decks*
And the sea is dotted
With little flecks
Of foam; like daisies
* gay;*

When there's salt on
* your lips*
In your eyes and hair,
And you watch
* other ships*
Go riding there,
Sailors are happy,
And birds fly low
To see how close they
* can safely go*
To the waves as they
heave and roll

Then, wheeling,
* they soar*
Mounting up to
* the sky,*
Where billowy clouds
Go floating by!
Oh there's fun for me
At sea
On a windy day!

A Windy Day,
Winifred Howard

NOTES

They that go down to the sea in ships,
That do business in great waters;
These see the works of the Lord,
And his wonders in the deep.

The Bible: from Psalm 107

I am fevered with the sunset,
I am fretful with the bay,
For the wander-thirst is on me
And my soul is in Cathay.

There's a schooner in the offering
With her top-sails shot with fire,
And my heart has gone aboard her
For the Islands of Desire.

I must forth again tomorrow!
With the sunset I must be,
Hull down on the trail of rapture
In the wonder of the Sea.

The Sea Gypsy, Richard Hovey